Carving Horses & Carriages with Power Tools

Carving Horses & Carriages with Power Tools

Billy J. Smith

Sterling Publishing Co., Inc.   New York

Library of Congress Cataloging-in-Publication Data

Smith, Billy J.
    Carving horses & carriages with power tools / Billy J. Smith.
       p.   cm.
    ISBN 0-8069-6954-7
    1. Wood-carving—Technique. 2. Power tools. 3. Horses in art.
  4. Carriages and carts in art. I. Title. II. Title: Carving
horses and carriages with power tools.
    TT200.S54   1989
    731.4'62—dc20   89-37759
                                         CIP

Copyright © 1989 by William J. Smith
Published by Sterling Publishing Co., Inc.
387 Park Avenue South, New York, N.Y. 10016
Distributed in Canada by Sterling Publishing
% Canadian Manda Group, P.O. Box 920, Station U
Toronto, Ontario, Canada M8Z 5P9
Distributed in Great Britain and Europe by Cassell PLC
Artillery House, Artillery Row, London, SW1P 1RT, England
Distributed in Australia by Capricorn Ltd.
P.O. Box 665, Lane Cove, NSW 2066
Manufactured in the United States of America

Dedicated to Doris, my wife of 40 years, for relieving me of the housewife duties most of my retired friends have to perform. This gives me almost unlimited "shop time" and the complete freedom to buy the tools I seem to always think I need.

Acknowledgments

To Howard Godfrey, my woodworking friend and neighbor, for the resawing, woodturning, and friendly prodding for perfection and for introducing me to Mesa, Arizona, Fire Chief Don Johnson, who furnished me with his toy fire engine and library of fire books.

To "Whittlin' Bill" Higginbotham for his good books and friendly encouragement and advice.

To the friends and family who have given me the praise and encouragement to keep at the carving.

All photo credits to Robert A. Schultz, Robin Photographic, Apache Junction, Arizona.

Contents

Preface

If we could meet, I'm sure that we would have a great visit! The fact that you are reading this book tells me that we have a mutual interest in woods and horses. It seems that once those two loves bite us they never leave, no matter how involved or how proficient we become as woodworkers or real horsemen. I have never met anyone who was infected with either love whose company I did not enjoy.

My father was a horse trader before he became an Iowa farm-equipment dealer in the mid-1930's. He took horses in trade on nearly all of the tractors he sold for several years, and he kept me in ponies and saddle horses until I left home. The most excitement my little hometown could offer was when the eastern horse buyers came to look over the 70 to 80 head Dad kept on hand. He was never without horses and had nearly 30 ponies when he passed away.

In 1948, when Doris and I were married, she was a city girl and totally afraid of horses. I never became a really good horseman but we continued to show at all the northeast Iowa shows we could get to, until the children started arriving. When they became teenagers we were back at the shows every Sunday of every summer weekend. Randy, like his dad, never became a really good horseman, but his love for horses will never dim. He has our collection of bronze horse sculptures in his bank office and has read and collected every issue of the *American Quarter Horse Journal* since the early 1960's.

Our daughter Maureen was a very good rider, but she preferred to let her brothers and mother take care of the horses during the week so that she could get dressed up on Sunday, ride her horse in the class, win, and then wait until the following Sunday to do it all over again. She has never lost her interest in and love of horses.

Our second son, Russ, started riding stick horses as soon as he could walk and has never stopped riding. He started training neighbors' ponies when he was 11 years old and quit college wrestling (his main reason for going) after two years to stand a young quarter horse stallion named Skip's Brick, which I had purchased as a long yearling in 1968. Russ showed Skip to his AOHA Championship and watched with pride as the young stallion made the list of AOHA leading sires for many years. While Russ's horse business was growing beyond our wildest dreams, Doris was helping him in all phases of the business and overcame her fears to become another true horse lover.

While Doris and I are still inactive partners, Russ's wife Roxanne has taken over for Doris, and their children Riley and Raquel are starting to win at horse shows. Russ has judged horse shows in most states in the U.S., Canada, Alaska, Germany, Brazil, and Italy and has sold horses in many foreign countries.

The reason for going into this family history is to point out that you do not have to be a professional or even a very good horseman to learn to admire and love these noble animals.

I have always regretted that I had no training in drawing or art; but over thirty years of drawing, engineering, and selling commercial buildings, farm buildings, and farmstead feedlots gave me lots of hours at a drawing board. When I sold my business in 1981, I bought some shop tools and started building furniture for ourselves, our children, and then friends and neighbors. This has taught me to love and respect fine woods and the things that can be done with them.

In late 1986, my daughter-in-law Kathy encouraged me to carve some Santa Clauses to add to her collection. I had worked some with clay, but the thought of making a mistake with a sharp knife (one I could not correct) made me afraid of carving. I have never been able to get my wife's kitchen knives sharp. I knew that I could never get a knife sharp enough to carve wood.

After reading everything I could find, I bought a Dremel tool set and a flex cable and drum sanders for my radial arm saw. The Santas turned out great!

Then, I enlarged a small photo of a carousel horse that was advertised and started sanding. My wife and friends were all impressed with the results and encouraged me to do more. *Wham!* Here was a hobby that brought my love for drawing, horses, and wood together. Five craft-shop lessons gave me enough ideas to put attractive paint jobs on the carousel horses.

Since then I have bought some great books on carousels and the pictures gave me inspiration for decorations. After I had made a few horses, I needed a place to display them, so I built a carousel. Plans for that are in this book. Then I made a stylized horse from a picture of an antique weather vane and hitched him to a racing sulky.

I thought a team of these trotters would look great on a steam fire engine. My neighbor (a great woodworker!) introduced me to our local fire chief who had an antique toy fire engine. I just put it on paper and made it. The chief then gave me three books full of pictures of antique horse-drawn fire equipment. By using composites I drew and built a ladder wagon and fire-hose cart. Plans for these are also in this book.

A friend from Chicago saw these wagons and commissioned me to build a beer wagon and hitch for his new Micro Brewery Restaurant, and I have included these plans in the book.

I hope you have as much fun with these plans and patterns as I do. If you have a problem, write to me, care of my publishers, and I'll be in touch. Let's get together and talk horses or wood or *both!*

1
Choosing Woods

The patterns in this book could be made from nearly any type of hardwood and finished to display the beautiful grain. I was told, however, and have frequently read, that the best carving wood is basswood. I have used basswood for everything that I have made except for the horses on page 37, Illus. 37 and 38, which are made of jelutong and in Illus. 32, 33, 59, and 60, which were made with wormy butternut.

Basswood has worked well for me. Jelutong is nice to work with but seems softer and is a little more expensive. Wormy butternut is a little harder than basswood, but I did not find it any harder to carve with my power tools. I doubt if you will find a better wood than basswood, especially if you are going to paint your project.

I try to buy boards about 7 or 8 inches wide. The carousel and harness horses can be made from boards 1⅝″ to 1¾″ thick. You should use 1⅞″ to 2″ thick boards for the draft horses.

Since you will be rounding the bodies from a center line down the back of the horse, the size of your horse will be larger when you use the thicker boards. If these thicker boards are not available, you can of course laminate thinner boards to the thickness you desire.

You will need a package of bamboo food skewers which are available at many grocery shops. The ones which I have are ³⁄₃₂″ in diameter. They come in 8″ and 12″ lengths and are inexpensive. I find them indispensable in building wagons and carts, and they can be used as gluing dowels when gluing parts together. You will need a supply of ⅛″, ³⁄₁₆″, and ⅝″ soft-wood dowels.

For the wagons and carts you will need a supply of ⅛″, ¼″, and ½″ thick boards. My neighbor has a wide blade in his bandsaw and resaws these for me, but I believe most hardwood shops would do this for you if asked. I have a 10″ Ryobi surface planer which is ideal for getting the thickness I want.

2
The Power Tools

In addition to the usual band saw, drill press, jointer, and table saw, I use my radial arm saw as the center of my carving area.

Illus. 1 shows the setup I use with the radial arm saw. The chuck and flex shafts are available at nearly all hardware outlets. The 3450 RPM of the motor has been just right for me to do the rough carving with the 1″, 1¼″, and 2″ drum sanders.

Illus. 2 shows my most frequently used tools. As you know, there are countless tools to choose from, and I have bought many of

Illus. 1. Arrangement for radial arm saw.

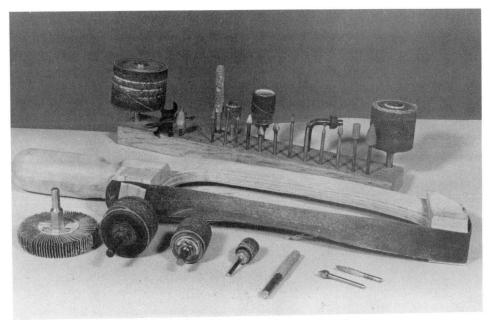

Illus. 2. Here are the most frequently used tools (see list).

them. My favorites may not be the same as yours, but I believe you have to just keep trying until you find the ones that work best for you. Here is a short description of the tools in the photograph:

1. 2″ flap sander wheel.
2. 1¼″ drum sander.
3. 1″ drum sander.
4. ½″ drum sander.
5. ½″ × 2″ tungsten carbide burr (silver).
6. Dremel steel acorn-shaped cutter.
7. Tungsten carbide burr—⅛″ shank (silver).
8. Handmade bow sander.
9. 2″ drum sander.
10. Chuck wrenches.
11. Tapered stones—⅛″ shank.
12. Tapered ruby bit.
13. Ruby bit.
14. Ruby bit.
15–17. Dremel steel cutters.
18–21. Ruby bits.
22–23. Stone tools.
24. Tungsten carbide burr—½″ × 2″ (gold).
25. ½″ drum sander.
26. ¾″ drum sander.
27. Chuck tool.
28. 1½″ drum sander.

Tools numbered 1–8 are the principal tools I use. With these few tools, I can get the rough cutting details and finishing on most projects in this book.

Using both a Dremel and a Black & Decker Hobby tool (bought used for only $15) saves a lot of time in changing tools. A homemade tool rack holds the tools in a handy position. The two lights and the shop vac hose in the lower left-hand of the picture complete this work area which I used until recently, when I changed to the setup shown in Illus. 3.

I recently built a dust collection box from scrap ¾″ plywood which is shown in Illus. 3 and 4. It is 18″ high, 18″ deep, and 24″ wide. In the back lower left-hand side, I drilled a 2½″ hole to receive the plastic tube from my shop vac. I made a 3″ × 3″ shelf and tapered the front to 1″ to allow the dust to pass under.

Additional shelves hold tools and supplies.

Illus. 3. Tool rack.

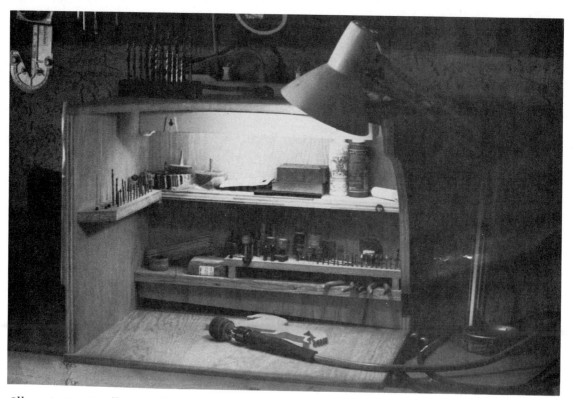

Illus. 4. Dust collection box.

Illus. 5. A set-up like this is extremely practical.

An 18″ single-tube fluorescent and the adjustable light with a 60-watt bulb give me enough light to work with. My Sears 16-gallon shop vac does an adequate job of pulling the dust, but I will eventually use squirrel-cage fans behind a dust filter to both give me better dust removal and less noise.

I seldom used my wood-turning lathe (and not very well when I did); so I removed the head and drive section and now use it to run the flex shaft for my ¼″ shaft tools. I set the speed at 3450, the same as the radial-arm-saw speed, and it makes an excellent drive.

A removable box over the chuck acts as a shield and a support for the Dremel tool. The addition of another Black & Decker hobby tool gives me four different tools to work with without changing tools. Illus. 5 shows the setup. If I were going to change it, I would make the shelf/shield taller and wider so that all three hobby tools would set at the same level.

3
Carving the Horse with Power Tools

Step by Step

The procedures discussed in this chapter have been developed in the course of making nearly 100 horses. They are not hard and fast rules, and I seem to find new shortcuts every time I make one. You may find new tools and methods that work better for you, but these have worked for me, and I believe they will work for you.

The main trick in carving a horse is to carve away everything that isn't a horse. (I think Michelangelo said something like that, only he said it better.) Each part of the horse is connected to the next part and it all flows together.

As I sand the horses down, I keep reminding myself to find a starting point and then round and blend from that point to the next part. Every part of the horse is round and smoothly connects to the next part. I start with a center line down the horse's back and round and blend everything off from this starting point. Really, the only places where there are dividing lines are the jaws and

flanks, and these have to be well defined to make the horse look real. The numbers in the following instructions refer to Illus. 6, 7, and 8.

1. Use clear tracing paper for your pattern. I have shown the off-side leg and hip positions with dotted lines and these will be of value to you when marking out your horse on wood. Select the style of horse you want to carve. From these few patterns you can make an infinite number of variations in the horse you make. By moving your tracing paper from pattern to pattern you can select the leg positions, head-setting, mane type, tail and foretop.

Remember that in the United States, carousels travel counterclockwise so that the outside rows of horses are always the show horses. The right-hand side of the carousel horse is called the "romance side." Thus the flowing manes and fancier decorations should always be on the right-hand side. In Great Britain, however, the reverse is true.

16

Illus. 6. Marking out the blank—Sides.

A. Draw the center line completely around the horse.

B. X-out the sides of the legs to be removed (see text).

C. Draw in the jawlines.

D. Draw in the outline of the mane you have chosen.

E. Draw in the outline of the saddle you have chosen.

Illus. 7. Marking out the blank—Front and rear.

A. Draw an inverted V and X-out the area to be removed between the rear legs.

B. Draw an inverted V and X-out the area to be removed between the front legs.

C. Draw in the face and ears (see text) and X-out the areas of the head to be removed. X-out the side areas of the head to be removed.

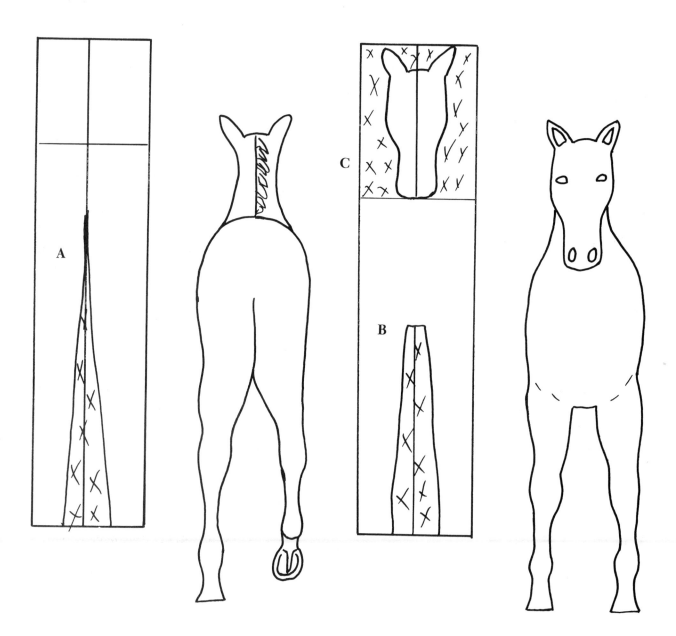

When you have your pattern completed on tracing paper, trace it on your board with carbon paper. Your board should be at least 1⅝″ thick for a carousel horse, 1¾″ thick is better, and you should use at least 1⅞″ thick boards for the draft horses.

Since you are going to "round and blend from the center line," the thickness of the board will determine to a great extent the overall size of your horse when you are finished.

Carousel horses were made a little thinner than real horses so that children could straddle them in comfort. You will have far less leg breakage if you can trace the horse on the board so that the grain runs up and down the leg. You will probably break some legs off anyway (I often do) but they are easy to glue back solidly, if you use a short piece of ³⁄₃₂″ bamboo skewer dowel. When the joint is sanded and painted you will never find the break.

2. Marking out the blank. When your horse is cut out on the bandsaw make a good dark line down the center of the blank from the tip of the nose to the center of the back legs. Draw center lines down the chest to the front feet. Do the same on the belly or underside (see Illus. 6A, 7A, 7B, and 7C on pages 17 and 18.

Then X-out the offside legs (Illus. 6B) and turn the horse over and X-out the opposite two legs. If you are making a team of horses, be sure to X-out the opposite set of legs so that the horses will not be in perfect step and look manufactured or cast when they are hitched. If the two right legs are extended, then the two left legs will be together on a trotting horse.

On the rear of the horse draw an inverted V (7A), starting just below where the tail will be attached later. You will be rough-sanding the legs down to this line; so do not get the legs too narrow at this point.

Draw the inverted V for guidelines on the front legs (7B).

Draw the rough guidelines for the face and ears (7C). Start with the jawlines: these should be halfway between the center line and the edge of the board. In other words, the distance between the jawlines should be ½ the thickness of the board you are using. The lines of the muzzle should be about halfway between the center line and the jawline. Taper the muzzle lines up to the jawlines.

Mark the ears, starting at the top of the jawlines as shown. (Illus. 7C) Now, X-out the areas of wood that will be removed. This helps while you are sanding.

You should also mark out the lines of the mane you have chosen. If it is a flowing mane, you will have to leave wood in that area to carve in the hair.

Turn your horse around in different positions and X-out any areas of wood that you will remove in the first rough carving. You will hold the horse in every possible position while you sand, and it is easy to lose sight of where you are carving if these areas are not well defined.

3. Rough carving. Begin by putting a 1½″ medium-grit drum on the flex cable of your radial arm saw. You may, of course, use your drill press, a portable drill, lathe, or even a separate motor; but I will describe using the radial arm saw since this is what I use. I push the saw's arm out of the way and set the Dremel tool with a medium-grit ½″ drum so I can reach the table. I put a #121 Dremel acorn-shaped cutter in my Black & Decker hobby tool and set it so that it will also reach the work. Then (and maybe most important), I lay the suction end of my shop-vac hose on the table so that it will draw the sawdust away from the work as I sand.

The bulk of the sanding at this point is done with the 1¼″ drum, but the ½″ drum and the acorn cutter are there to get in tight spots. Obviously, you need only one hobby tool and can change tools, but I was lucky enough to "steal" my Black & Decker at a garage sale for $15. Illus. 1 on page 12 shows this tool set up. At the end of this chapter there is a photograph section which shows most of the following steps.

4. Sanding with the 1¼″ drum. Start by rounding the back and saddle seat from the center line out until the back and top line rounds and blends into the body sides. You can then round the belly in the same way so that you now have the rounded barrel of the body.

Now round the outside edges of the hips and blend them into the rounded back. Just round the hips (or breeching) down to about where they will meet the tops of the legs.

Now lay the horse on the worktable and sand the sides of the head down to the guidelines, which define the jaws and muzzle.

When the rough square shape of the head is obvious, you blend the neck back down to the back and join them. Leave enough wood for the mane if you have one.

The horse's neck is narrow (or almost pointed) on top and becomes gradually wider as it goes lower. You can round the bottom of the neck and blend to the chest. You may need to use the ½″ drum or acorn cutter in this area at this time, depending on the head set of your horse.

Now lay the horse on the table and sand off all of the Xed-out portions of the legs. You may want to use a smaller drum for this, and you will have to use a smaller drum for the upper parts of the legs.

You now have a roughly rounded body and hips, head, neck, and chest and four square legs. Change your tool to either a ¾″ or 1″ drum with fine grit.

5. Sanding with the ¾″ fine-grit drum. Always put your sander drum on the rubber so that it protrudes out over the end of the drum. This will let you use the outside end of your drum for marking and defining lines. With your pencil draw in the jawline, neckline, saddleline, and the flanklines both front and rear.

Define the jawline and blend the neck on down to the body and down and around the chest.

Define the neckline and blend the neck down and around. If you prefer, you can cut the hairlines in the mane now with the end of your ½″ drum. Just cut deep V's with the tool. You can also cut these with the acorn cutter.

With either your ¾″ or ½″ drum define the outline of the saddle (if there is one) and blend out from this line to the rest of the body.

Round the muzzle and blend this up to the jaw (just get the rough round shape) and round off the forehead. You will finish the head and ears later.

Now start rounding the outsides only of the legs. Be sure that they blend with the body at the top and come straight down at the same width as the body. Shape the legs so that the knees and ankles are large and obvious—you will finish these later.

6. Finish carving with your Dremel tools. I have bought and tried nearly every hobby tool offered, and I am down to just a few that I use. Most frequently used is the ½″ drum sander (mostly fine grit). I like the Dremel #121 or #124 acorn-shaped cutter. With a little practice you will be able to cut straight lines, drill various sized holes, and cut in tight places with it.

20

I have some Carbide Kutzall cutters that work well. A silver BN14 bullnose ¼″ dia. × 1½″ is alright for rough-cutting large areas. The gold-colored T18E with a ⅛″ × ¾″ head is a very nice tool for smooth cutting between legs, and so forth. It is tapered and good for tight spots. The DN14 is a gold-colored bullnose ¼″ × 1¼″ and it is a nice smooth cutter. I have two diamond cutters: a #5 tapered and a #11 small round that are nice to use in tight spots. Another practical one is a regular-grit ruby carver #17.

In spite of the fine small finishing tools, I still do most of the carving with the ½″ drum. With this drum, finish rounding the muzzle and blend it into the jaws and neck. Then blend the neck down to the chest, shoulders, and back. Round the forehead and blend this to the jaws.

Use the drum sander to shape the ears. Use the acorn cutter to drill out the ears from the front. With the drum sander you can flatten out the areas where the eyes and nostrils will go. Drill the nostrils with the acorn cutter and drill the holes where the animal eyes will be installed in wood filler, after the horse is painted. Be sure these holes are horizontal with each other and large and deep enough to receive the eyes. You will have to use the small tapered tools to clean up the areas around the throatlatch where the head meets the neck.

Using a combination of the cutters described above, clean out the areas between the legs both front and back and blend up to the chest and rump.

You have the outsides of the legs rough-shaped; now turn the horse upside down and draw the shoes on the bottoms of the hooves. Drum-sand to this shape. Now turn the horse right side up and you have the starting point for blending the legs back up to the body. Start by shaping the hooves, then the pas-

terns, ankles and fetlocks and keep rounding and blending and tapering the legs until they are blended in with the body.

Using the small tool of your choice carve the horseshoe and frog on the bottoms of any feet that are raised and turned to where they will show when the horse is finished. Remember that the lower leg between the knee and pastern is flat and that the upper leg tapers out from the knee and is very muscular.

Using the small diamond cutter or an acorn cutter, you can carve the lips of the horse, leaving the teeth exposed.

Define the flanks both front and rear. You will notice that the legs run up into the body at all four flanks and you will want to round the belly up to these flanks.

7. Making the tail. Choose a tail that matches the action of your horse from Illus. 8; on a piece of scrap wood about 1½″ square and 2–3″ long, draw the profile and the top of the tail on your wood as shown in Illus. 8. You can change the shape of the tail very easily with your markings. Bandsaw it both ways and then sand it round. Now with the ½″ drum cut deep-flowing V's the length of the tail as shown. Hold it up to the proper location on the horse and sand the upper end to conform with the shape of the hip at that point. Glue it on to the horse with a ³⁄₃₂″ dowel for support.

If you want real hair, you can get wig samples from most beauty salons. They come on a metal ring with about 24 colors so you can choose one to match your horse. The ones I use are the perfect length, and I just drill a hole in the horse the same size as the metal end holding the hair. Push the metal end in the hole and fill any void with wood filler.

By gluing some hair together you can also make hair foretops.

If you want a wooden foretop, you can make

it the same way in almost any shape that fits the horse. (See Illus. 8)

8. Finish-sanding of the horse is done first by using a ½″ wide × 2″ diameter flap sander in the radial arm saw flex cable. You can get at most areas with this, and it will smooth it down pretty well. When I get everything done that the flap sander will reach, I finish the sanding with a homemade bow sander (see Illus. 25). This will reach nearly all areas and is great for the finish-sanding.

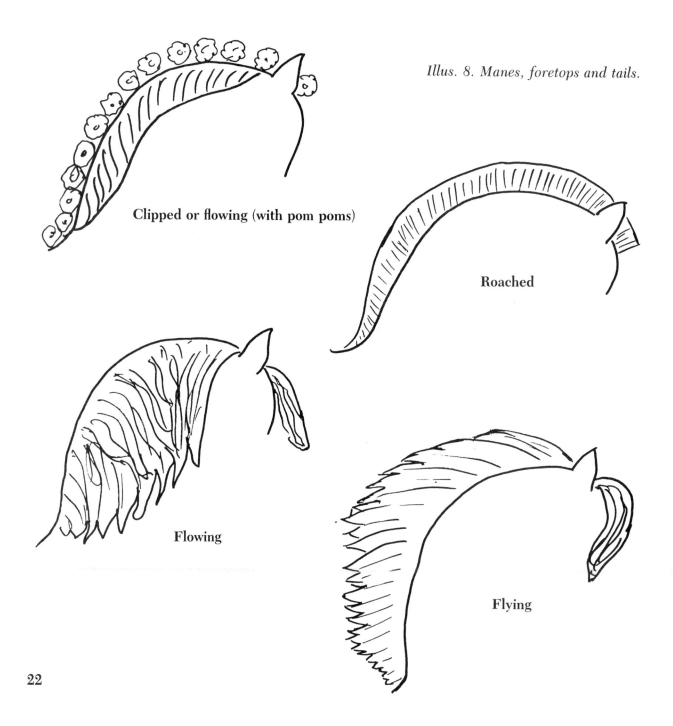

Illus. 8. Manes, foretops and tails.

Clipped or flowing (with pom poms)

Roached

Flowing

Flying

22

FORETOPS

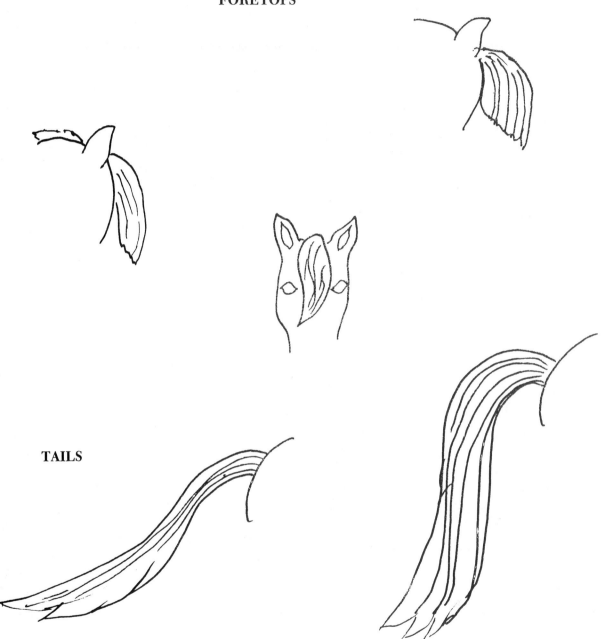

TAILS

23

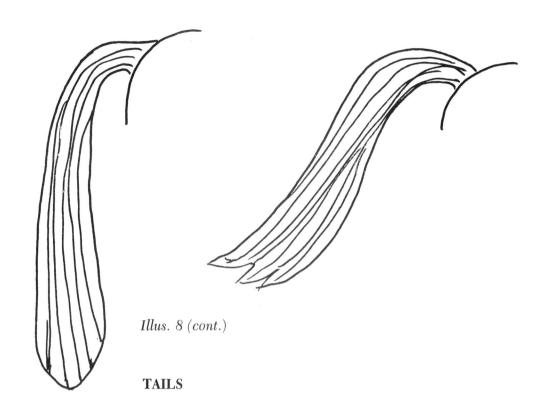

Illus. 8 (cont.)

TAILS

Side

Top

9. Drilling the support hole. Using a 6"-long, 3/16" drill, drill the pole hole as near the neck as possible. The hole is important and should go as straight up and down as possible when it is viewed from the front of the horse. When looking at it from the side of the horse, the angle can make a big difference in the horse's appearance. On a standing or prancer type of horse, the body should be pretty level; but on a trotter, jumper, or cantering horse, the withers or front shoulders should be higher than the rear. On horses that are going to be hitched, you just drill from the bottom up, being careful to get the right angle.

Step by Step in Photos

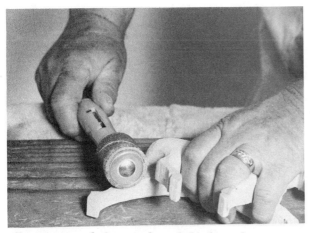

Illus. 9. Sand the insides of the legs down to the Xed-out lines with a 1¼" drum sander.

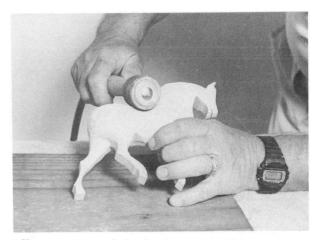

Illus. 11. Round the back, neck and hips with the 1¼" drum.

Illus. 10. Rough-shape the head by sanding down to the lines you have drawn on the face.

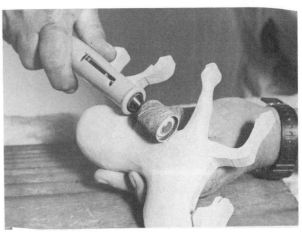

Illus. 12. Define the flanks and jaw with a 1" drum.

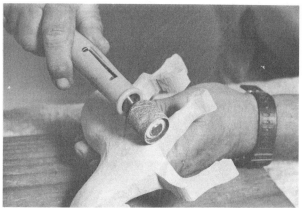

Illus. 13. Round the rump and the outsides of the legs. Be sure to leave the joints large; you can refine them later.

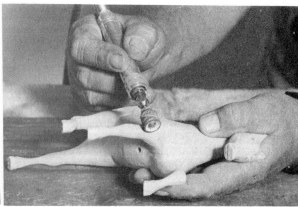

Illus. 15. Finish with your Dremel tools: With a ½" drum, complete the insides of the legs and finish rounding the outsides. Note how the joints in the legs are smoothed to blend with the rest of the legs, but are left well-defined.

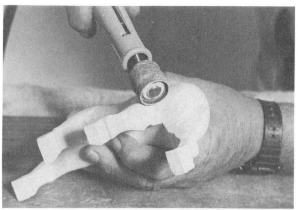

Illus. 14. Start to round the front of the neck and blend down to the front leg. Shape the outside of the leg, again leaving the joints large.

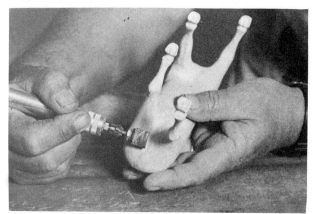

Illus. 16. Smooth out and sand the V-line up to the rump with the ½" drum.

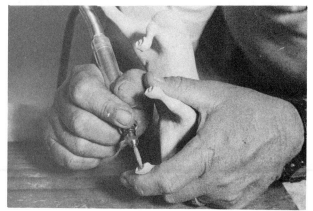

Illus. 17. The Cutzall tool carves the frogs and shoes on the bottoms of all hooves that will be exposed.

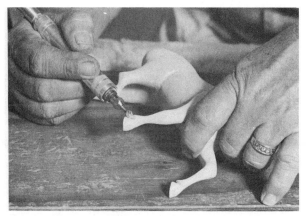

Illus. 18. Shape the fetlocks with the acorn cutter. This can also be done with either the ½" or the ¼" drum sander, depending on the size of the horse's legs.

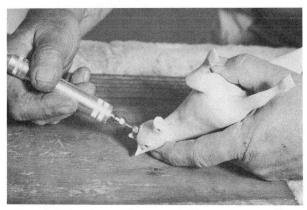

Illus. 19. Drill the eyes, nostrils and ear fronts with the acorn cutter or a Cutzall tool.

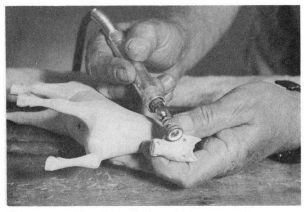

Illus. 20. Note that the area between the ears has been done with a ½" drum sander. The backs of the ears are smoothed and blended to the head with the same drum.

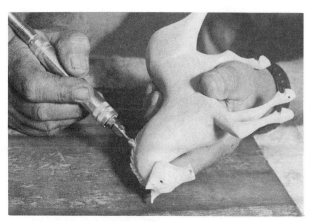

Illus. 21. Cut the mane in with an acorn cutter or drum sander.

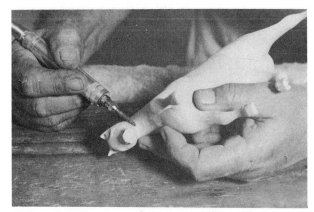

Illus. 22. The Cutzall tool gets into tight areas where other tools won't go.

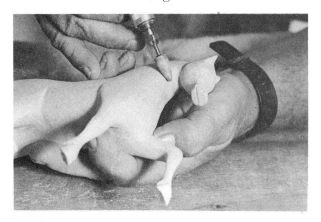

Illus. 23. Finish the head with the ½" drum and grinding stone.

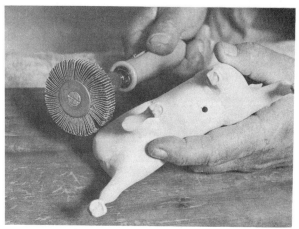

Illus. 24. The flap sander starts the sanding on all areas it can reach.

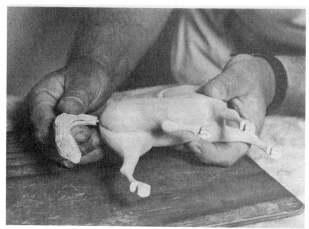

Illus. 26. The tail is glued in place and your horse is then ready to paint.

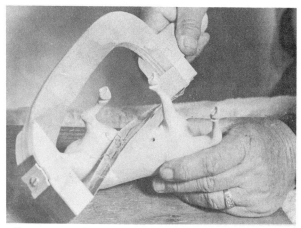

Illus. 25. A bow sander will get into areas that your flap sander cannot reach.

4
Painting and Finishing

Later, you will find brief descriptions of how each horse and wagon has been finished. This chapter covers the general instructions and tools for the few simple designs that I have used. The tools shown are available in any good art supply shop except for the dowel, which is made by just cutting off a regular ¼″ dowel. In addition to these, I use permanent pens in the colors that I need (I prefer Pilot brand). For paint my favorites are the plastic flip-top bottles sold by Delta Technical Coatings, El Monte, California. I have lots of colors I seldom use, but you will find that black, white, yellow, red, flesh, 2–3 shades of green, and 2–3 shades of blue and gold are necessities. You may also want a small bottle of accent silver metallic paint.

I use regular spray-paint cans to put the

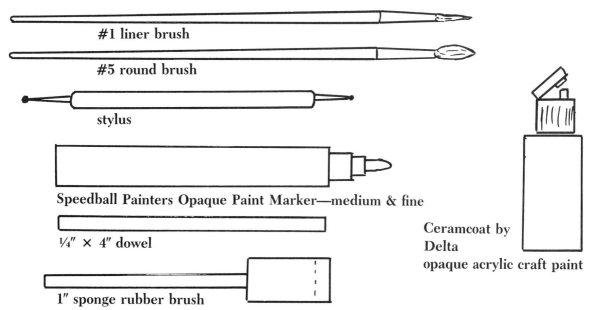

#1 liner brush

#5 round brush

stylus

Speedball Painters Opaque Paint Marker—medium & fine

¼″ × 4″ dowel

1″ sponge rubber brush

Ceramcoat by Delta opaque acrylic craft paint

Illus. 27. Brushes, markers and paint bottles.

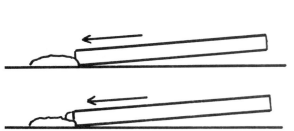
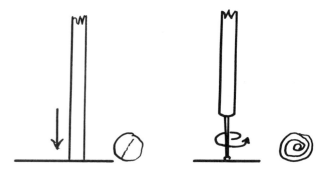

Illus. 28. Painting a rose.

first or basic colors on. Most brands work equally well but I like Accent Country Colors. They have nice soft "country" colors, particularly their #384 JoSonja Red for the fire wagons. Get at least one can each of white, black, gold and clear satin varnish. You can save a lot of time and do a good job of final finishing with either a spray varnish or a clear matte.

The designs shown in the following illustrations are simple to make and I don't think you have to be an artist to master them. Practise them on a sheet of paper and I am sure you will find them to be easy and fast to make. They will give your work that professional look. As the old saying goes. "Your friends and neighbors will be amazed!"

Painting a Rose

There are several simple steps in painting a rose: Start with a small puddle of red and a small puddle of yellow (or any other two compatible colors).

1.) Push a 3″ to 4″ piece of ¼″ dowel into one of the puddles until one half of the end is well covered with that color.

2.) Turn the dowel over and cover the other half of that end with the other color.

3.) Deposit the paint where you want the rose and you will have a slightly oversized circle of ½ red and ½ yellow paint.

4.) Use your stylus and make about three swirls to mix the paints together and you have your rose.

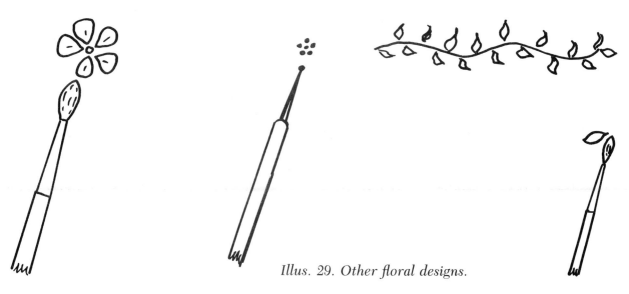

Illus. 29. Other floral designs.

Be sure to get enough paint on so that it leaves a nice clear swirl mark when you use the stylus. If you do not have nice deep puddles, the colors will not mix well.

Petal Flowers are made with a #5 brush, as shown. Use a bright-colored dot in the center to represent the seeds. These can be any size that you need.

Daisies are made with the stylus. Simply make five dots in a circle and then use a contrasting color for a dot in the center.

Vines fill up space fast and are easy to make. Draw a wavy line to represent the stem with a fine-point permanent pen (dark green or black). Add the leaves.

Leaves are also simple to make but you may have to practise a page of them with your #1 brush. Simply load the brush, touch it down heavily near the stem and lift and pull it off the paper or wood. Think of them as commas— round spots with tails. They seldom come out the same but it would not look natural if they did, because you are looking at them from all different angles. Use at least two shades of green. Do about half of your leaves in one color and then fill in the other leaves with the other shade.

Wagon Trim Designs

Curlicues are made with a soft tip or fine or ultra-fine permanent pen, depending on the size you need. The old wagon painters used curlicues liberally in any length or size.

Wheat flows (there is probably a better name for these) are made with the stylus. Load the stylus with paint and it will make about 8 dots and each will be progressively smaller.

Dolly Parton hearts are made with a stylus or a ⅛″ or ¼″ dowel, depending on the size you want. The three easy steps are shown: 1. Put two dots side by side. 2. Reload the stylus and put a third dot below the pair. 3. Fill in the sides with the stylus, as shown.

Dot borders are made with the stylus and used to accent borders in many places, such as around the edge of saddles, on the edge of wheels, etc. When you want a row of bolts, use metallic silver.

Line border every area you are going to paint. It gives an area a framed look and makes your finish look professional. Any wagon side or distinct area needs to have a border as close as practical to the outside edge.

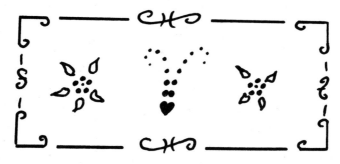

Illus. 31. Examples of combinations.

Corner designs were used by many wagon painters to accent the corners of an open area that they were going to paint. I use a plastic square template to make these. I use a plastic circle template to paint all circles.

These few little designs should be easy to master, and adding them in some combinations of your choice will give you the professional finished look you want. Do not be afraid to mix and match colors! Illus. 31 shows samples of some combinations you might want to use.

Patterns for the horses and carousel are in chapter 5, starting on page 33.

The pattern for this pull-toy cart can be found in Illus. 50, page 46.

This grey runaway's pattern is Illus. 58, page 52.

B

See pages 84 and 85 for the plans for this fire-hose cart.

Plans for this sulky and driver start on page 75.

The story behind this adaptation of a William Jauquet design starts on page 78.

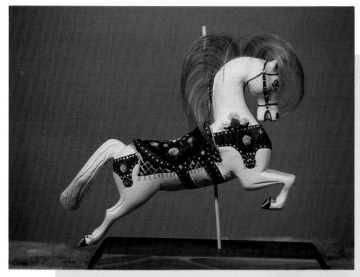

A piece of an old wig makes a fancy mane on this flyer. The pattern is in Illus. 41, page 40.

The popular Parker flyer pattern for this Country Fair type of horse is Illus. 53, page 48.

Illus. 36 provides the pattern for this flyer, which was carved from jelutong and finished in clear varnish.

Another view of the carving on facing page. Instructions for finishing this carousel horse are to be found in chapter 5.

A lock of my grand-daughter's blond hair provided the tail of this Charles Looff copy. The pattern is Illus. 61, page 54.

Like the Looff flyer above, this horse was carved from wormy butternut with a natural finish.

E

Headin' for the smoke! Plans for this engine are on page 93.

Hurryin' to the big picnic! Build your own beer wagon from plans starting on page 113.

Here come the ladders! See page 101 for plans on building this ladder wagon.

5
Building a Carousel

Before you can build a carousel you have to have horses to put on it. The two horses in Illus. 32, 33, 34, and 35 were made from the same pattern in Illus. 36. They are typical Coney Island style, sometimes called jumpers. The manes, tails, colors, saddles, and angles of the poles make them appear very different.

Illus. 32. Can be seen in color on page C of color section.

Illus. 33. Another view of the horse in Illus. 32.

Illus. 34. Can be seen in color on page B of color section.

Illus. 35. The flying mane was made from a wig.

The horse in Illus. 32 and 33 was made from butternut and then sprayed with a clear matt finish. Then the mane, tail, foretop, teeth, and two of the socks were painted white. The saddle was painted brown and decorated with roses, leaves, and dots. Small tassels were painted around the saddle. The breast collar, bridle, and hooves were painted black. I used a very simple breast collar so that it did not distract from the grain. Two or three coats of the clear matt finish were sprayed on after the painting was done. This is one of the last carousel horses that I made, and it shows progress from earlier ones.

To paint the saddle blankets, I draw the outline with a pencil. You can use almost any shape and color that you desire since the blankets are all individual and really look better if they are not perfectly aligned with anything. By sweeping the back corners towards the rear of the horse, there is an effect of more action. Paint your basic blanket color first, then with either a soft-tipped red paint marker or #1 liner brush color lines diagonally to make it appear to be plaid. Paint a border line and tiny tassels around the edge of the blanket.

Draw the breast collar and bridle with a pencil and then paint in your basic colors. Use a contrasting color to border them. Multicolored rhinestones were used to border the bridle, saddle, and breast collar as you can see in Illus. 32 and 33.

The flying mane on the horse in Illus. 34

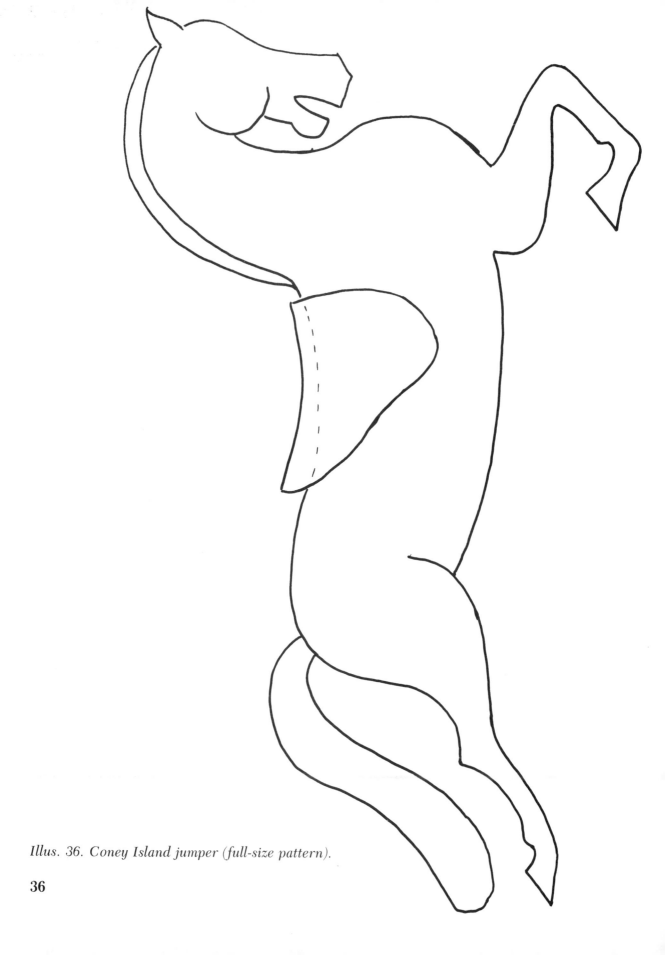

Illus. 36. Coney Island jumper (full-size pattern).

Illus. 37. In color on page C of color section.

and 35 came from an old wig which I bought at a garage sale. I just cut a strip of the wig and glued it on. The saddle seat was painted a dark color and covered with flowers and vines. The wide breast collar and the double belly bands on the saddle give lots of room for decorations. The dotted borders are easy to make with the stylus and accentuate whatever they are used on.

Paint silver horseshoes on any hoof that is turned up or exposed.

I had found four "jewelry store" roses and put them on the breast collar and painted the rest. The roses just above the breast collar on the neck are satin ribbon roses.

The eyes on both of these horses were painted and done before I discovered animal eyes at the craft shop.

The bases on these horses (and many others in the book) are walnut boards that have been cut to a 15-degree angle on all four sides and stained and varnished.

The horses in Illus. 37 through 40 on pages 37–39 are also Coney Island styles, sometimes referred to as Jumpers. They both were made from the pattern in Illus. 41 and have one front foot extended, but I moved the right rear foot forward on one of them. The palomino color in Illus. 37 was achieved by spray-painting him gold. I custom-made this horse for a lady who wanted the blue colors in the saddle and liked the wig mane. The English saddle and breast collars are covered with flowers, vines, and rhinestones.

The neck and throatlatch on the black horse in Illus. 39 and 40 is sanded down so thin that it is almost abstract, but the nice part of working with carousel horses is that they are fantasy horses anyway, so it gives you freedom to change some of their conformation to suit

Illus. 38. This one is in color on page B of color section.

Illus. 39.

Illus. 40.

yourself. The bridle tassel was made from a short piece of plastic cord string. Just drill a hole, insert it and fluff out the end.

I like to put stocking legs on my horses and use strips and bald faces on the heads. The stocking legs look more natural if you do not try to make the tops of them stop evenly. The very deep cuts on the tail were done with a drum sander in the Dremel tool.

The pattern in Illus. 41 provides several head positions from which you may choose. You might find it a little easier to carve if you use one of the extended heads on your first few horses.

The horses in Illus. 42 through 49 are called "prancers." They were usually mounted on the carousel with three legs solidly on the platform and one front leg extended. All of

these horses were made from the pattern in Illus. 50. This was the first pattern that I ever made, and Illus. 41 is the first horse that I ever made. Since doing these, I have learned that it is much easier to do the tails separately. You can do a much better job around the rump area and give the tails more action. These pictures illustrate the different appearances you can get by just changing the colors and decorations. Actually, this is what the old carousel carvers did. They did not have a large number of patterns but made small changes to make them appear to be different horses.

On the white horse in Illus. 48 and 49 I painted a sort of cross-stitch design on the saddle to give it the appearance of being quilted. The pull-toy wagon is just a ¼" board with wheels, but it makes a different way to

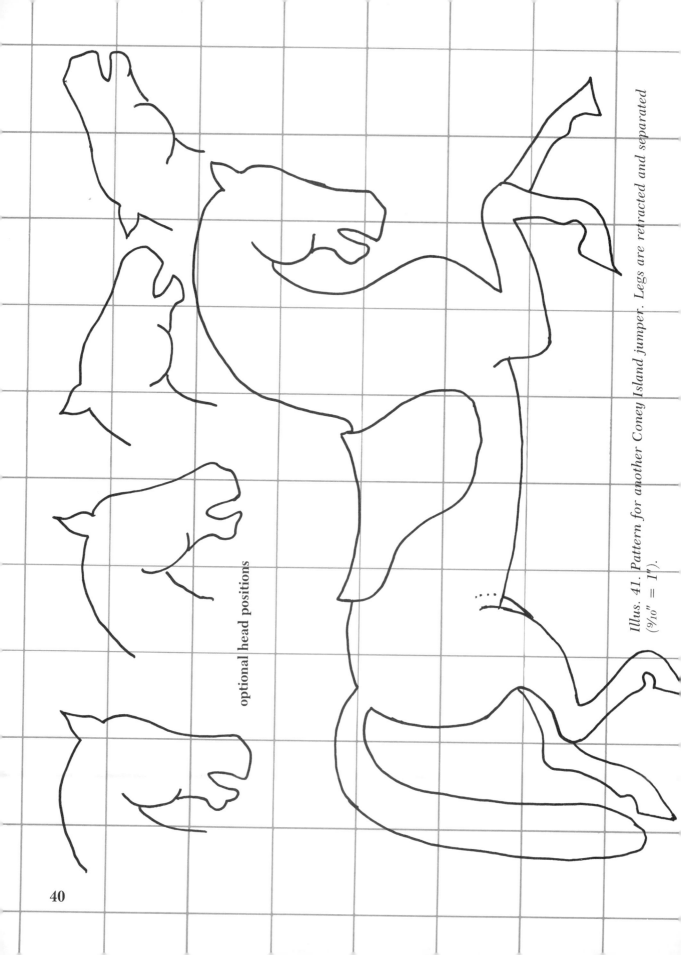

optional head positions

Illus. 41. Pattern for another Coney Island jumper. Legs are retracted and separated ($^9/_{10}'' = 1''$).

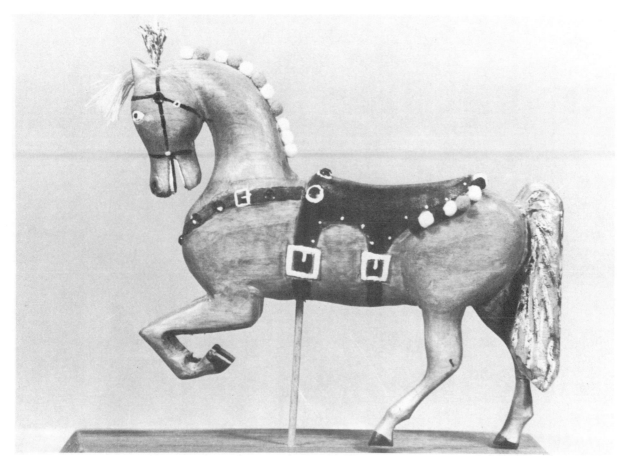

Illus. 42.

display your carving. The belt buckles on the saddles were just painted on, and I had no craft shop decorations when these were made. The pompons and a few rhinestones were added later.

The pattern in Illus. 50 shows you both the English and western saddle. You can change the head set by using Illus. 41 and change the tail by using Illus. 8.

The horse in Illus. 51 and 52 was made from the pattern in Illus. 53. Charles W. Parker, who carved carousel horses in Abilene and Leavenworth, Kansas, from 1894 until 1925, used this horse in many variations. Many of his horses had flags and other patriotic decor. He first introduced this horse in about 1916 and continued to use it until he stopped production.

Parker preferred to use the "bob-tailed" type of tail. You can use this or add a longer tail.

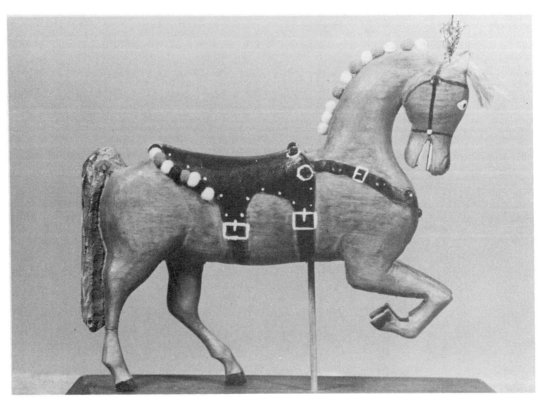

Illus. 43.

Illus. 44.

42

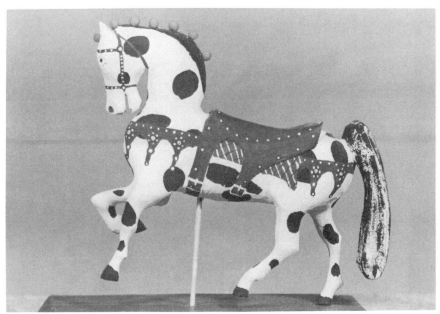

Illus. 45.

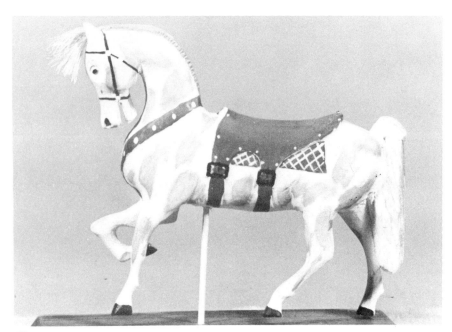

Illus. 46.

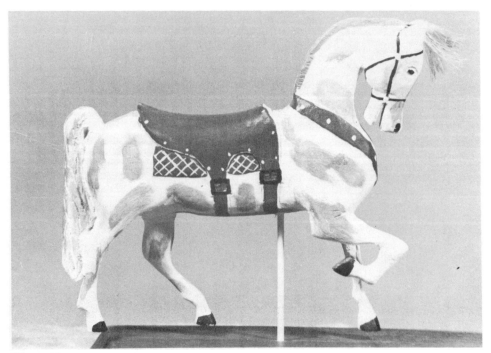

Illus. 47.

Illus. 48. In color on page D in color section.

44

Illus. 49.

This particular pattern will make a slightly smaller horse than the previous patterns, but the Parker Company made many "Country Fair"-type carousels with smaller horses so that they could be easily transported. Notice in the picture how the foretop wraps around the right ear.

The horses in Illus. 54 through 57 are made from the pattern in Illus. 58. This is a versatile pattern that can be used for a horse rearing, on a cart as a harness horse, or on a carousel as in Illus. 54 and 55 by simply changing the angle of the pole.

The grey color is produced by spray-painting the horse white if you want a white mane and tail or black if you want the mane and tail black. Then you mix black and white paint to get the grey you want and dab it on the horse with a porous sponge to provide a dappled effect.

There is more about carts in the following chapter. I was going to carve a driver for this horse, but I felt that it would distract from the horse; so I just carved a little skunk and glued him behind the cart to make it appear that the horse had lost his driver from fear and was running away.

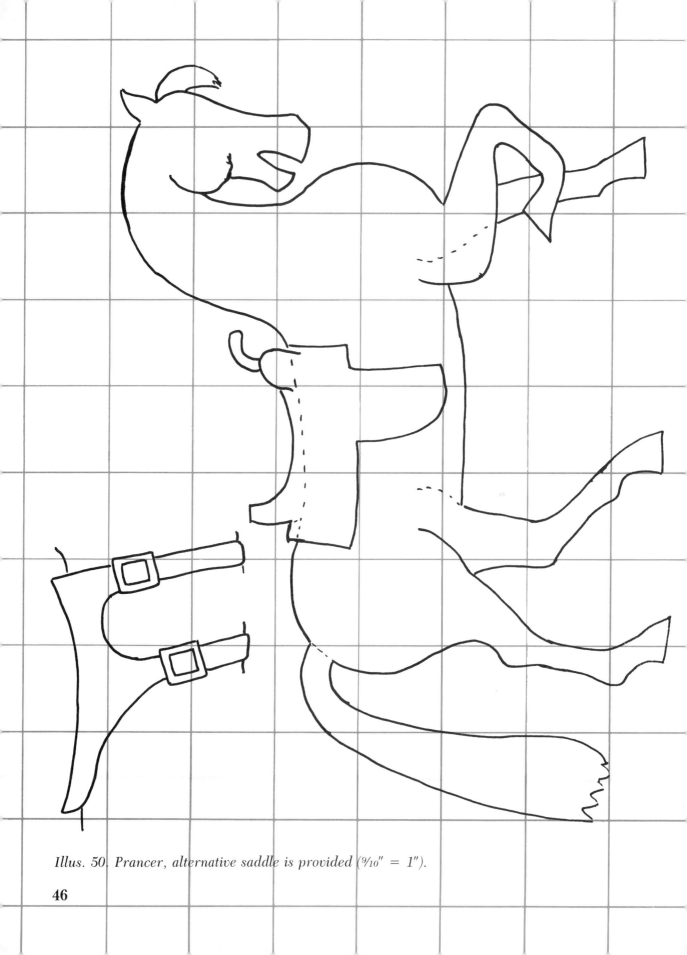

Illus. 50. Prancer, alternative saddle is provided (⁹⁄₁₀″ = 1″).

Illus. 51.

Illus. 52. In color on page B of color section.

Illus. 53. Country fair style (full-size pattern).

Illus. 54.

The foretops on these two horses were both carved and fitted to the heads. The color on the carousel horse was achieved by using an oak stain and wiping it off more in some areas than in others.

The horse in Illus. 59 and 60 was carved from wormy butternut and finished with several coats of a clear spray varnish. The tail was made from a lock of my granddaughter Erin's hair. I plan to make horses for Trisha and "Kelly" whenever they go to short haircuts and send me the locks.

Many carousel horses had real horsehair tails, and I think these will make nice and attractive keepsakes for my granddaughters!

Charles Looff, who built and installed the first carousel on Coney Island, New York, in 1876, carved the original of this horse after he moved his factory to Long Beach, California in 1910. It was done before his death in 1915 and has been restored and is now in a private collection. Illus. 61 is the pattern for this horse.

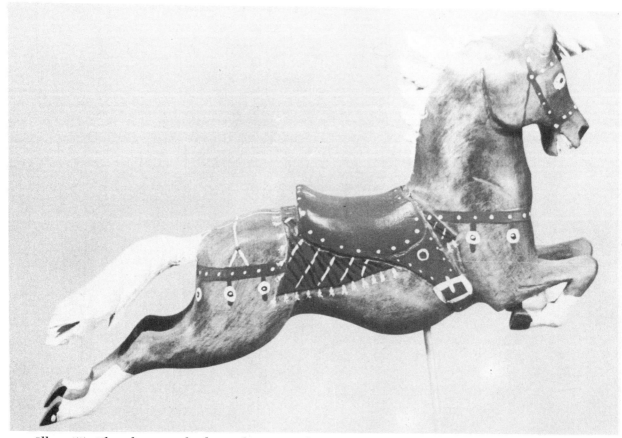

Illus. 55. The photograph above shows another view of the horse shown in Illus. 54. This horse and the one shown in two views on the opposite page along with the one in color on page D of the color section are all made from the pattern in Illus. 58 on page 52. This demonstrates the many variations that can be achieved from the same pattern.

The circus horse in Illus. 62, 63, and 64 makes an interesting variation on a carousel. The grey dapples are done with a sponge.

Circus people use a minimum of decor on these horses so that it will not interfere with the rider.

Illus. 56.

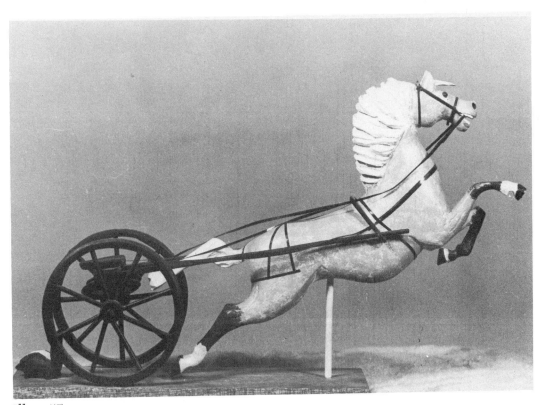

Illus. 57.

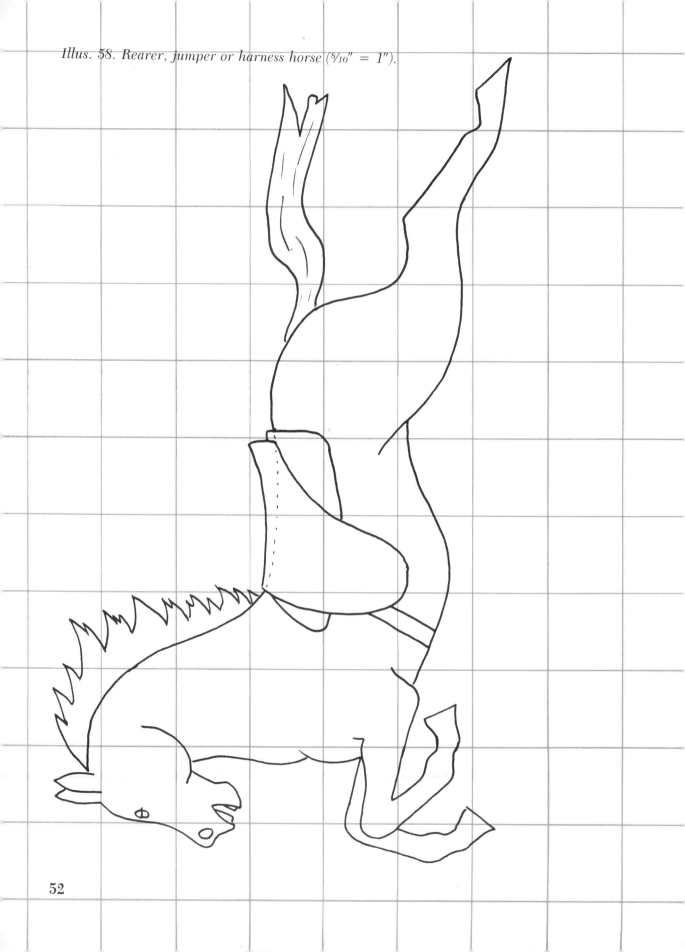

Illus. 58. Rearer, jumper or harness horse (⁸⁄₁₀″ = 1″).

Illus. 59.

Illus. 60. The horse shown in two views on this page can also be seen in color on page C of color section.

Illus. 61. Jumper—Coney Island style (⁸/₁₀″ = 1″).

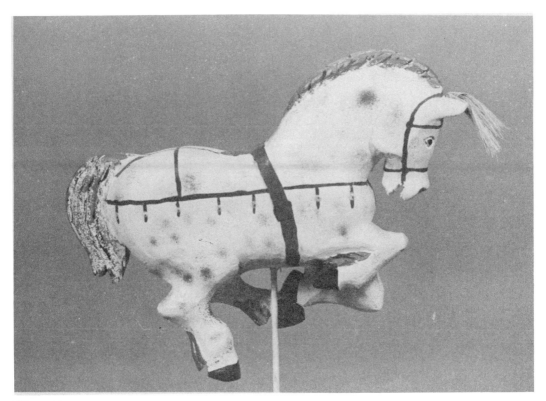

Illus. 62.

Illus. 63. Two views on this page of a circus horse.

Illus. 64. Circus horse (full-size pattern).

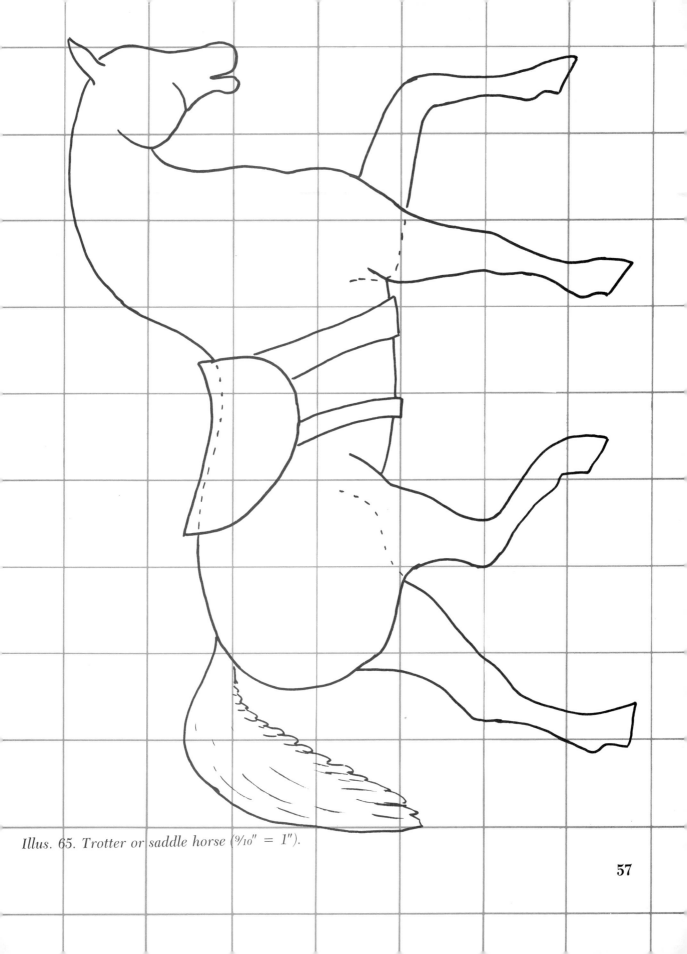

Illus. 65. Trotter or saddle horse (⁹⁄₁₀″ = 1″).

The horse patterned in Illus. 65 is a well-balanced saddle horse. He is probably better suited for a light harness horse or in a buggy team but could be used as a carousel horse also. You could use nearly any mane, head, or tail position to change him.

This sample carousel is easy to make and is an ideal way to show off your first six horses. I used a plastic, revolving cake tray for my base but have drawn these plans with a lazy susan bearing. It could be mounted on an electric revolving tray similar to the ones jewelers use for display. You may want to use a refrigerator turntable instead of the lazy susan bearing. I got one at the local hardware shop, but they should be available in most places. The 10½" × ¾" size is ideal. They are low cost and you can eliminate the base (Illus. 69A) in the plan.

Following are some suggestions that should help you assemble the carousel shown in the plans in Illus. 69 and 70:

Illus. 66. Carousel: Different views on page 59 and 60, and in color on page A of the color section.

Illus. 67.

THE CAROUSEL

Number	Description	Thickness	Width	Length
A.	Base	½″	18″ dia.	
B.	Platform ring	¼″	18″ dia.	
C.	Platform	¼″	18″ dia.	
D.	Top	¼″	18″ dia.	
E.	Center Panels	¾″	3″	11½″
F.	Panel Stand	½″	7″ dia.	
G.	Center Pole	¼″	dowel	24″
H.	Horse Poles	³⁄₁₆″	dowels	16″
I.	Rounding Board	⅛″	1½″	57″
J.	6″ Lazy Susan Bearing			
K.	Cloth Top			

Illus. 68.

1. The base (Illus. 69A) platform (69B) and (69C), and top (69D) are all made from ¼″ plywood. Put the five pieces together and saw them all to 18″ diameter.
2. Glue two pieces together to form the base (Illus. 70A).
3. Saw about a 14″ diameter center out of one piece to form the platform ring (Illus. 69B) and glue it to the platform piece. This will form the cavity for the lazy susan bearing.
4. Next saw two pieces of ¼″ plywood to 7″ diameter and glue them together. This is the panel stand (Illus. 69G). Drill a ¼″ hole in the center.
5. Double-tape the platform (Illus. 69B) and top (69D) together and drill a ¼″ hole in the center and 6³⁄₁₆″ holes around the edge about 1″ in from the outside edge.
6. Cover the edges of the base (Illus. 69A), platform (69B), and panel stand (69F) with wood edging tape.

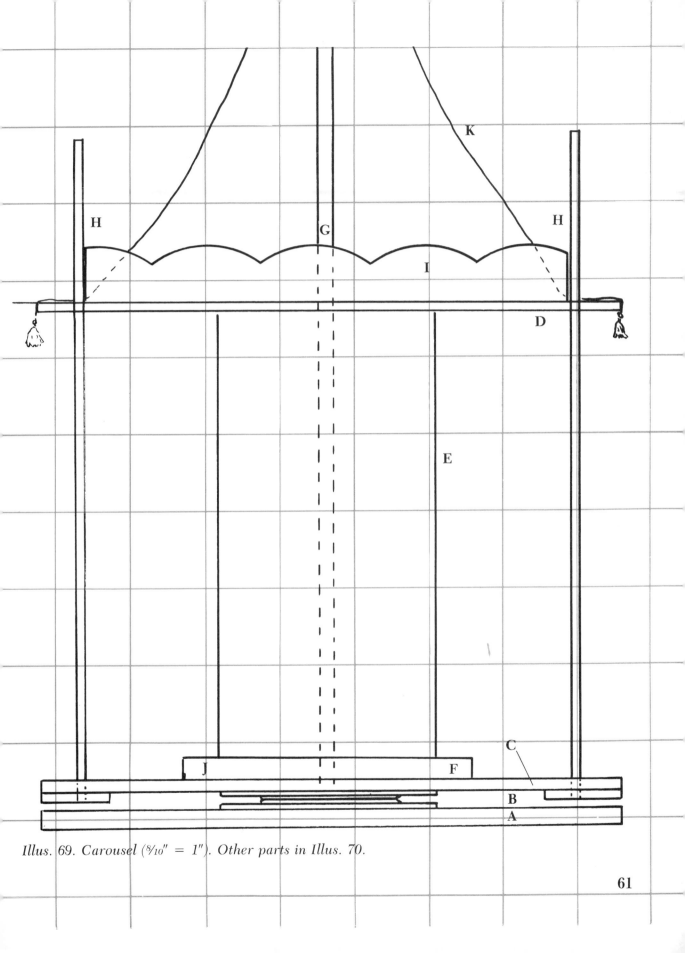

Illus. 69. Carousel (⁸⁄₁₀″ = 1″). Other parts in Illus. 70.

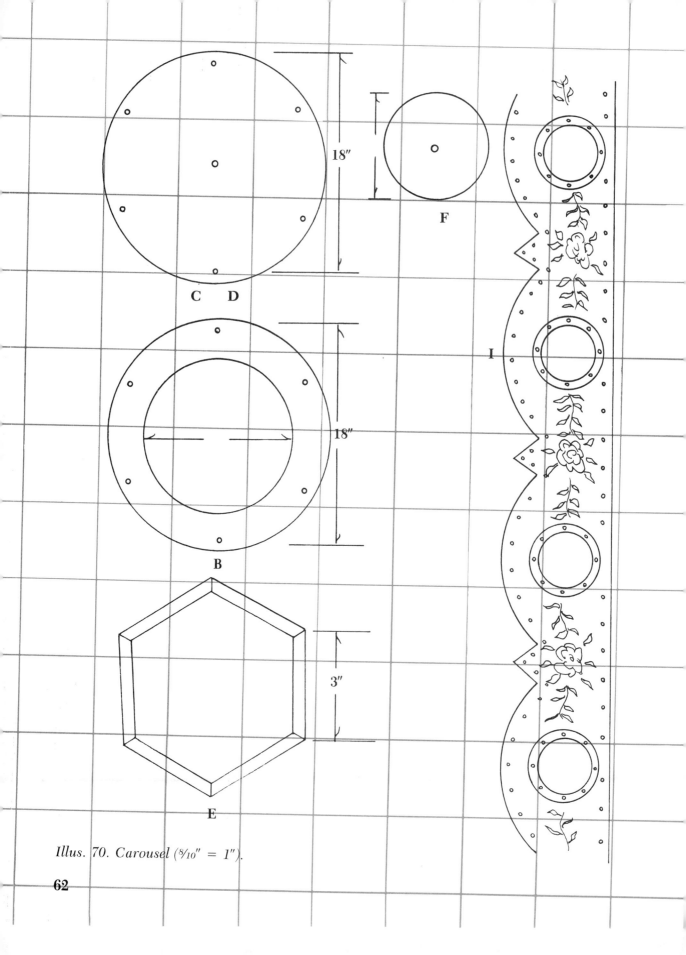

Illus. 70. Carousel ($\frac{8}{10}$" = 1").

7. To make the center panel (Illus. 69E) cut six ¾″ boards 3″ × 11½″ long and then saw the 11½″ edges to 30-degree angles. Glue them together and stain all the wooden assemblies before completely assembling the carousel. Glue mirrors or other decorations on the center panel.

8. To make the rounding board (Illus. 69I), cut a piece of hardboard or Masonite 1½″ wide and at least 57″ long. This should be too long, but when you assemble it you will either overlap the ends or cut it to the correct length so that it will lie just inside of the protruding horse poles. I used ¼″ plywood for mine and cut the back so that it would bend, but a bending board would be easier. Using the full-size pattern in Illus. 70, cut a scalloped edge on one side. Paint it white. Using a circle template and a red permanent soft-tipped pen, I drew the ¾″ and 1″ circles as shown.

The craft shops have ½″ round mirrors (very thin) and also filigrees. I glued the mirrors in these circles, but you could use filigrees. Put bright-colored dot borders top and bottom to represent lights and fill in the blank areas with flowers and vines.

9. We chose a red-and-white-striped material to represent the top canvas and used the white tassel edging shown in the photos. A seamstress friend of my wife's cut the material in triangles and made the top. You cut holes for the center pole and the horse poles, and it drapes over the edge of the top. The rounding board then sets loose on top of it and inside of the horse poles. Cut the poles to the desired length and put the flags on.

When you mount the horses, cut the poles at different lengths and just insert them from the bottom and top so the horses appear to be cantering (or are at different heights off the platform). I have never glued my horses in place, so I can interchange them if I want to add new horses. This also helped when I wanted individual photos of the horses.

6
Making Common Wagon Parts

This chapter includes plans and instructions for making common parts for use on the wagons discussed later in the book. The axles, wheels, springs, fifth wheels, neck yokes, tongues, double and single trees are interchangeable on the wagons and could be used to make wagons of your own design. I know of no place where you can buy any of these parts and there is a satisfaction to making them yourself.

The most difficult to make (and I can find no place to buy them) are authentic-looking wood-spoke wagon wheels. Without authentic wheels, your wagons never look complete. Here's an easy way for you to make the wheels. It is simple to change the number of spokes, sizes, and so forth. The plans will make 16 wheel rims at a time—4 each of the 4″ diameter, 3¾″ diameter, 3⅛″ diameter, and 3¼″ diameter: All letters refer to those on Illus. 71 on pages 64 and 65.

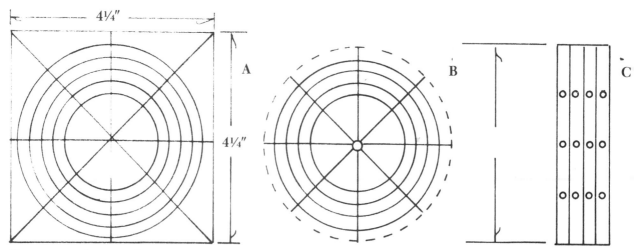

Illus. 71. Making spoke wheels (full-size).

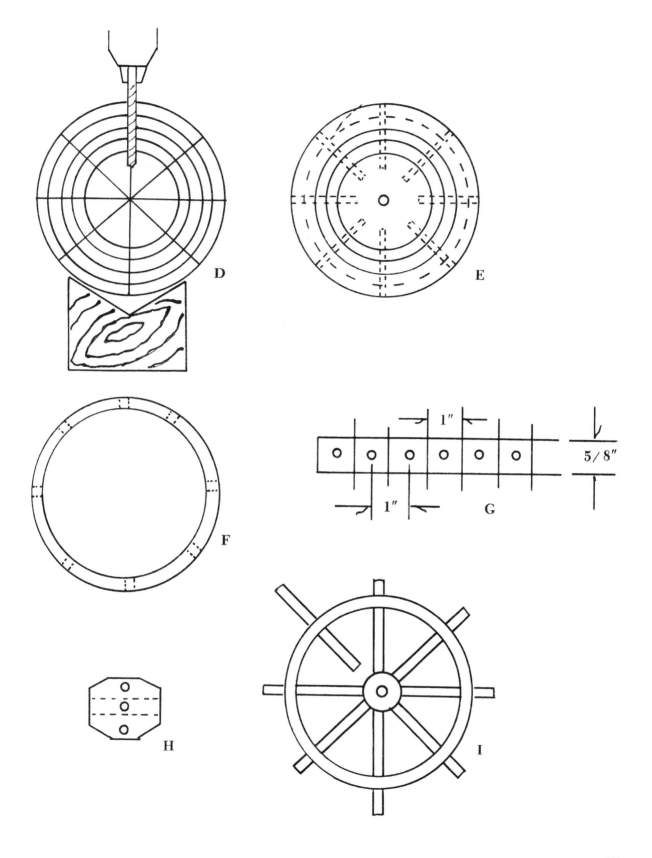

D

E

F

G

1"

1"

5/8"

H

I

1. Cut four ¼" thick boards 4½" × 4½". Fasten these, one on top of the other with double-faced tape (small nails near the center will work, but be careful not to locate them where the saw or drill bit will strike them). On the top board draw the pattern as in 71A.

2. Drill a ³⁄₁₆" hole in the center and insert a dowel (don't glue) so that it protrudes on one side about a quarter of an inch. This dowel holds the layers in place and can be used to hold them while sanding round. I have built a sanding table for my drill press so that after first sawing the 4-inch diameter, I can round the outside smooth and true. You might want to round yours on the belt of your disc sander or use any other method you have developed.

3. Using the spoke location lines on your top or pattern board, draw straight lines across the face of the circle to locate the spoke holes—see on Illus. 71.

4. Using a V-block on your drill press, drill the twenty-four ⅛" spoke holes as shown in 71D. Be sure that the drill goes deep enough to go through the inside 3¼" rim. *Note:* After you drill your first hole, make sure that your spoke dowels slide freely into the holes. If not, use the next size larger drill bit. These should slide easily for successful assembly and gluing.

5. Sand the outside of your disc lightly to remove any roughness from the drill bit, and then bandsaw on the dotted line as shown in 71E. Be sure to start your saw between two spoke holes.

6. You can now remove the four 4" rims. Glue the slot together and clamp with a small clamp. When the glue has dried, you can sand the kerf marks out of the inside of the rims with a drum sander in your drill press. These 4" rims are now ready for assembly to the spokes and hubs. Continue to cut, sand, and glue the 12 remaining rims as above. You will have to fill the areas where the rims are glued back together with wood filler and sand smooth.

7. On a ⅝" dowel about 18" long draw 6 equally spaced horizontal lines. The best way I have found to do this is to locate the lines at one end and then lay the dowel in the groove of my table saw and draw the lines horizontally from each mark using the table top as a pencil guide. Now draw lines around the dowel every 1". Where the lines intersect, you will drill a shallow hole with the same drill bit you used for the rims. When the holes are all drilled, you can saw between each row of holes and you will have ⅝" diameter hubs 1" long.

8. Drill a ³⁄₁₆" axle hole through the center of each hub. Place a 3" to 4" long ³⁄₁₆" dowel in the axle hole, and with your disc sander taper both ends of the hubs as shown in 71J.

9. Now completely assemble the rim, spokes (cut about a quarter of an inch longer than you need), and the hub. When you have adjusted it so that you are satisfied that the rim is as round as you can get it and the hub is centered as close as possible, slide one spoke out of the hub hole. Place glue on the spoke just outside the rim and on the hub end of the spoke and push it back in place. Do the same with the remaining 7 spokes and let the glue dry. Clip off the protruding spoke ends and sand until the spoke ends are flush with the rim. Sand the sides of the rims smooth on your belt sander and your wheel is complete.

Finishing: I spray-paint the basic color, then paint the "steel" rim black. You may need to use a little wood filler around some of the

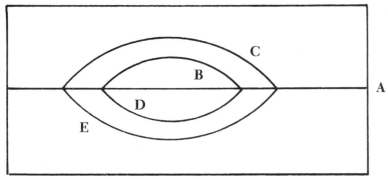

Illus. 72. Springs.

spokes. Paint the hub ends (around the axle holes) black. If you are like me you will slop some black on the sides of the rims. Touch this up with a brush.

Using your stylus, put silver dots on the sides of the rims about ⅜″ apart. Now paint a silver ring around the outside ends of the hub to represent a steel band.

Springs

To build leaf springs use ¼″ material at least 2″ × 3″. Each pattern will make one complete spring so use double-sided tape and make as many thicknesses as you need springs. By cutting these all at once, they will be the same size. Copy the pattern on your top board. Cut the pieces in 2 on line 1 and then cut 2 and 3 and then 4 and 5. You will want to round out the edges and sand out the kerf marks before gluing them back together. On heavy wagons (steam, ladder, beer, and so forth) the springs were mounted into a square with the ones glued to the axle running parallel with the wagon, and the ones glued to the fifth wheel or box running crossways. Paint the assembled springs black.

To build a neck yoke (Illus. 73), cut a piece ¼″ × ½″ × 2½″ and copy the pattern on it. Drill the ³⁄₁₆″ hole for the tongue to slide through. Cut it to the shape of the pattern and

round off the edges to make it basically round.

The evener (74A) is made from a piece ¼″ × ½″ × 3″. Drill the ³⁄₃₂″ holes as shown. Round the ends and sand smooth.

Illus. 73. Neck yoke.

The single trees (72B) are made from pieces ¼″ × ½″ × 2″. Drill the ³⁄₃₂″ hole and sand to the shape shown. Glue the single trees to the evener with ³⁄₃₂″ food skewers as shown.

Fifth Wheel

Building a fifth wheel. Fasten two pieces of ¼″ scrap wood together with double tape and draw the pattern in Illus. 75 on the top piece. Cut them out, drill a ³⁄₁₆″ hole at the center (+), and sand the edges smooth. Separate them and complete sawing the circle on the top piece (75K). By cutting and sanding both pieces at the same time, they will be the same size and shape. It is a good idea to mark them before you separate them so they can be mounted on the wagon in the same positions.

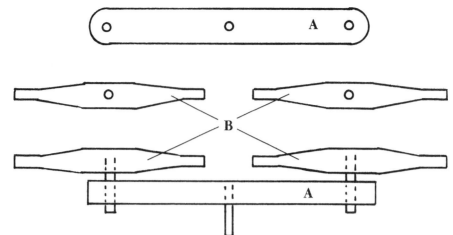

Illus. 74. Doubletree.

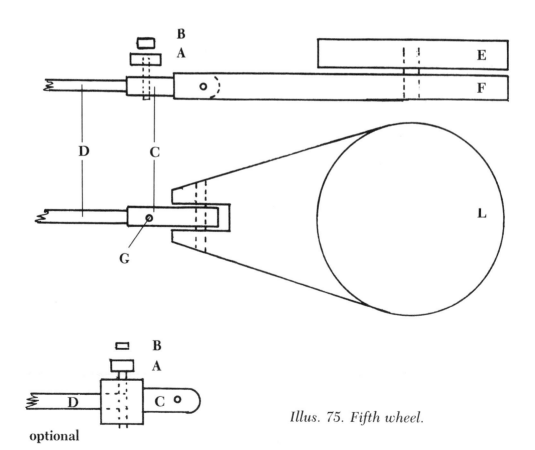

Illus. 75. Fifth wheel.

optional

Building a tongue. Saw a ¼″ × ¼″ × 1″ piece (Illus. 75C). Drill a ³⁄₁₆″ hole ¼″ deep in one end to receive the tongue (Illus. 75D) and the two ³⁄₃₂″ holes as shown to receive the doubletree and the pull pin that connects the tongue to the fifth wheel. Glue a 12″ long piece of ³⁄₁₆″ dowel (Illus. 75D) into the hole in (Illus. 75C). Do not cut this tongue to its proper length until you have your horses hitched to it. Attach the doubletree evener and singletrees (Illus. 75A) and (B) (see Illus. 74) to the connector (Illus. 75C) as shown.

You can also build the connector (Illus. 75C) from a ½″ × ½″ × 1″ piece as shown above as "Optional."

Axles

Building axles. Cut a piece ½″ × ½″ × 4″. Drill a ³⁄₁₆″ hole in each end. Determine and mark where the springs (Illus. 75) will be glued on and from these marks round out the center with a drum sander and taper the outside ends until they are just slightly larger than the axle holes. Glue a ³⁄₁₆″ × 1½″ dowel in each end.

For sulky and cart axles, you just make two axle blocks (Illus. 76H) ¼″ × ½″ × ½″ as shown in the rear and side view of Illus. 76. Drill a ³⁄₁₆″ hole in the center to receive the ³⁄₁₆″ dowel that will be the axle.

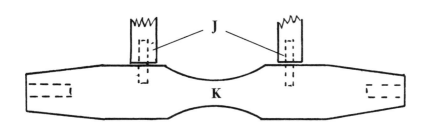

Illus. 76. Axles.

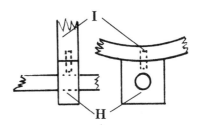

7

Harness Horses, Harnesses, and Carts

The horse in Illus. 78 and 79 was made from the pattern in Illus. 82. This stylized trotter must have been used on thousands of weather vanes and is still being used on the ones made today. This horse inspired me to make a team of them and put them on the fire engine wagon you will see later in the book.

I got a good bay color by painting him black

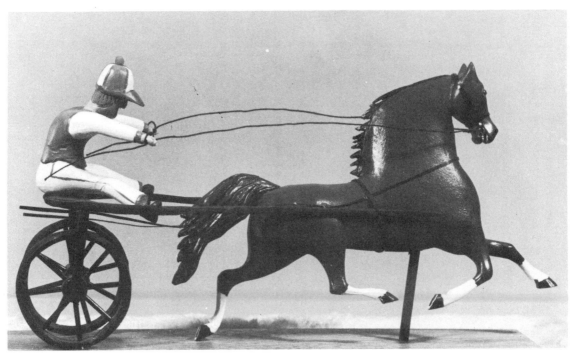

Illus. 77.

Illus. 78. Another view of the sulky and driver on the facing page. It can also be seen in color on page E of the color section.

and then mixing red and black until I had the bright bay color I wanted. Two coats of this and a coat of matt finish gave it an almost silky look. Four white socks and a stripe on his face set him off. The dotted line on the pattern shows an optional neck line.

The sulky is a take-off of the plan in Illus. 81 except that I left the springs off and made two forks and smaller wheels. I think I would like the sulky with the larger wheels like the one in the plans, but I have never taken time to change this one.

Building a driving harness. Any office supply shop has Chartpak (or another brand), pressure-sensitive graphic tape in various widths and colors. I use black ⅛″ width to make the driving harnesses. The following numbers refer to Illus. 79 page 72.

1. The breast collar and tugs (Illus. 79d) are a double thickness of the tape stuck to-
gether sticky side to sticky side. I clamp a nail out of my vise horizontally above the floor. I then pull out about 20″ of tape and bend it over the nail, and as I pull more off the roll of tape, I stick them together. This is a tricky job, but it can be done.

2. Put the tugs (Illus. 79d) in place on the horse and tape them there with 2 or 3 laps around the belly. This makes the belly-band (Illus. 79b).

3. Tape the breeching (Illus. 79c) directly on to the horse. I have painted this on some horses, but the tape looks better.

4. Tape the headstall (Illus. 79f) on the head. Tape the noseband (Illus. 79e), browband (Illus. 79d), and throatstrap (Illus. 79g) directly onto the head. I paint the bridles on some horses so I can get wider headstalls to decorate. I like the paint just as well as the tape.

71

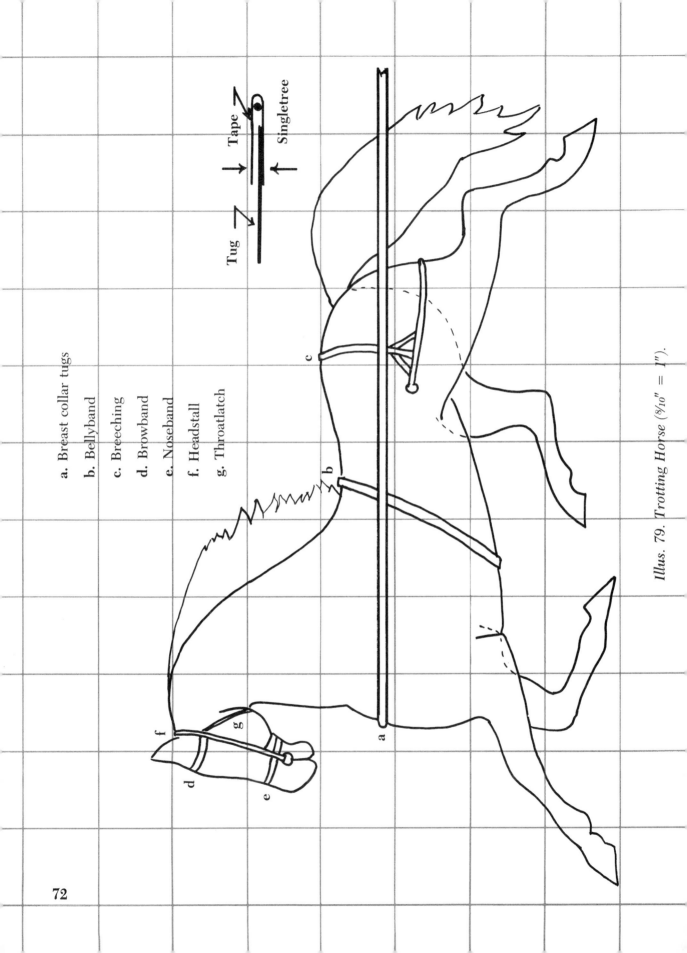

a. Breast collar tugs
b. Bellyband
c. Breeching
d. Browband
e. Noseband
f. Headstall
g. Throatlatch

Tug
Tape
Singletree

Illus. 79. Trotting Horse (⁸⁄₁₀" = 1").

5. See the draft horse harness in Illus. 91 on page 88 to make the bit and lines.
6. When your horse and cart are mounted on the base, cut the tugs just short of the singletree and tape it as shown in the sketch in Illus. 79. Since these were made, I have used jump rings (available at all crafts shops) to make the tug ends. They look great and will slide right over the ends of the singletrees with a little sanding.

UTILITY CART

A	Sides	2	¼″	1¾″	4″
B	Footboard	1	¼″	¾″	2½″
C	Floorboard	1	¼″	2½″	3¾″
D	Tailgate	1	¼″	½″	2½″
E	Seat Back	1	¼″	1½″	2½″
F	Seat Board	1	¼″	1″	2½″
H	Axle Blocks	2	¼″	½″	½″
M	Springs	4	¼″	See pattern	
J	Single-horse fills—see pattern Illus. 97.				

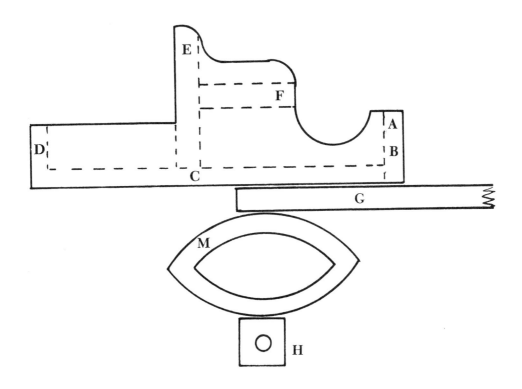

Illus. 80. Utility cart (full-size).

Building a Racing Sulky

Here's a very simple little cart to build and you can make all kinds of changes to suit your own taste. The letters in the following instructions refer to the plans in Illus. 81.

1. Using the pattern for fills (B) in Illus. 97 on page 95 make the fills from ¼" stock. Round the fills with your ½" drum sander. Round off the back corners.
2. Cut the seat as shown and hollow it out for the driver with your Dremel ½" drum sander and glue it in place on the fills.
3. Add the springs, axle blocks, axle, and wheels as described in Chapter 6 earlier.

Put a singletree (Illus. 74B) directly in front of the driver (not shown in the drawing).

4. You can paint a racing sulky any color or combination of colors that you choose.

Building a single-horse utility cart. You can build utility carts like the one shown in the plans in Illus 80 almost any way you desire. Make the box longer or shorter or eliminate it. Build it with or without springs. Simply make the fills (Illus. 97J) as patterned in Illus. 97 page 95 and go on from there. Paint it the color of your choice.

The trotting-horse pattern in Illus. 82 gives you another option for a harness horse.

Racing Sulky

Letter	Description	Quan.	Thick.	Width	Length
G	Driver's Seat	1	¼"	1¼"	1½"
H	Axle Block	2	¼"	½"	½"
I	Axle	1	³⁄₁₆" dowel		4¾"
M	Springs	4	¼"	See pattern	
J	Single-horse fills—see pattern Illus. 97.				

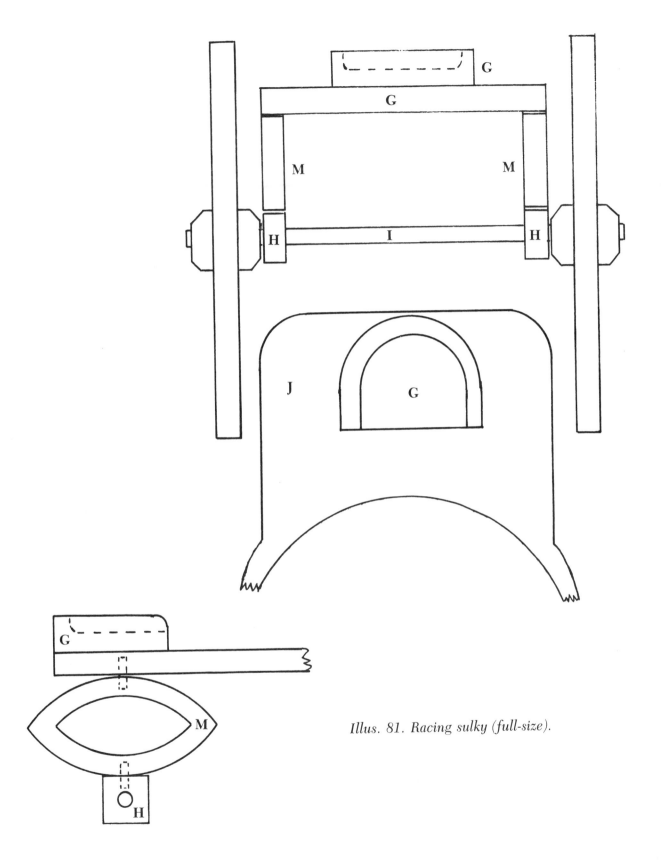

Illus. 81. Racing sulky (full-size).

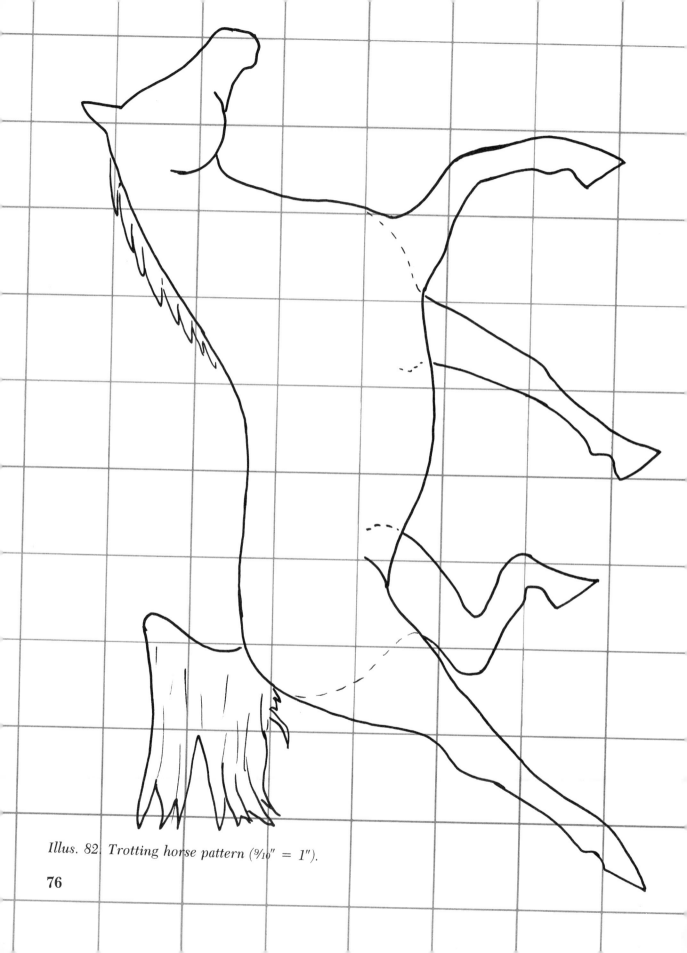

Illus. 82. Trotting horse pattern (⁹⁄₁₀″ = 1″).

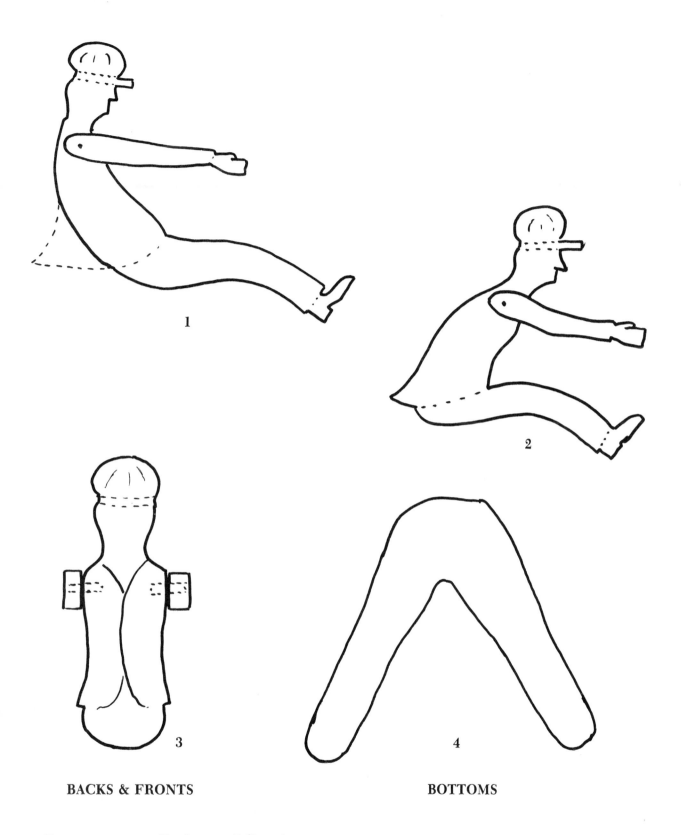

1

2

BACKS & FRONTS

3

4

BOTTOMS

Illus. 83. Racing-sulky drivers (full-size).

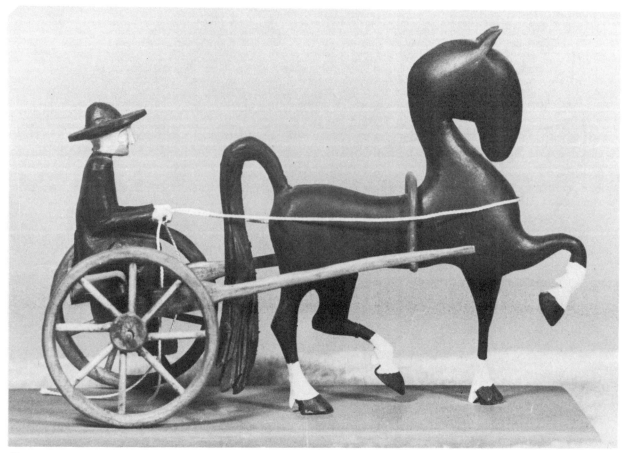

Illus. 84. My version of a William R. Jauquet carving.

I was first exposed to the carvings of William R. Jauquet when I read an article in the October 1985 issue of *Country Home* magazine. The pictures of his distinctive, stylized carvings impressed me; when I found that I too could carve a horse, I wanted to see if I could make one that looked like one of Bill Jauquet's. From a picture in that article I made the pattern in Illus. 86, and the figures in Illus. 84 and 85 show the results. This is obviously not a Jauquet carving (for one thing, it is less than a quarter of the size of his 56″ original), but it gave me a lot of satisfaction and its distinctive flowing lines draw lots of compliments from our visitors.

My wife and I visited Bill Jauquet in his studio near Denmark, Wisconsin this past summer. I showed him the original manuscript of this book and explained that I would like to use this pattern so that other carvers

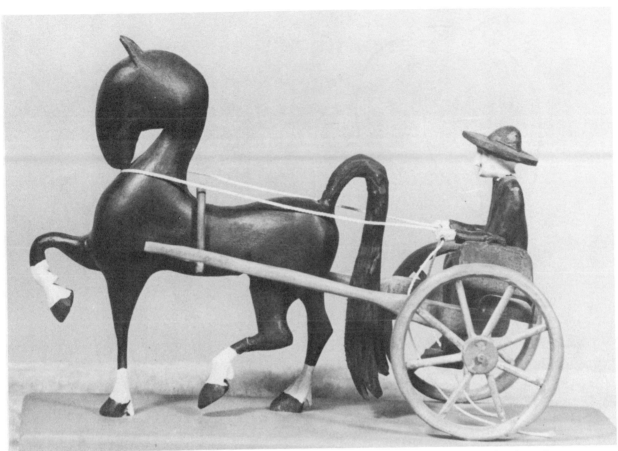

Illus. 85. Another view of the carving shown in Illus. 84. A color version can be found on page E of the color section.

might enjoy making a copy of one of his carvings. He graciously agreed, and we learned that this was typical Bill Jauquet. His rapid growth from a celebrated folk artist to a highly regarded fine artist has been nothing short of phenomonal. He has been featured in several magazines, has had showings in the Museum of American Folk Art in New York, has pieces in several museums including the Smithsonian Institution. He is now producing bronze castings with his own special patina, and these are being featured in the finest art galleries in the United States. Certainly he is one of the most important young artists in America today. The museums, galleries, and collectors have put the price of his work out of the reach of most of us, but a few hours with the proper tools and skill will let the carvers at least enjoy a copy of a fine piece of art—thanks to Bill Jauquet!

Illus. 86. From an original carving by artist William R. Jauquet, Denmark, Wisconsin. (Full-size pattern here and on facing page.)

Building a Single-Horse Hose Cart

Like other horse-drawn fire equipment, the hose carts all seemed to be designed differently. This cart is simple to make and represents the ones used around the turn of the century. The letters in the following instructions refer to the plans in Illus. 89 and the descriptions of parts in the table on page 83.

1. Double-tape 2 pieces of wood ¼″ × 1¾″ × 6″ together and copy the cart sides (A) on the top piece. Cut the sides out and drill the 2 ³⁄₁₆″ holes as shown.

2. Cut B, C, D, and E to size (plan is full-size—measure) and glue the body assembly together. You should glue the ³⁄₁₆″ dowel in the back of the body in at the same time. Paint the body red and put your designs on before gluing to the fills.

3. Cut the hose-reel sides (F) from ⅛″ stock 2½″ in diameter and drill a ³⁄₁₆″ hole in the middle of both. Paint them white and paint vines on the outsides.

4. Turn the hose spool (G) to 1½″ diameter and cut it to length that will make your hose-reel assembly not over 3⅜″ wide when the sides are glued on. You can use a length of 1″ or 1½″ dowel for this if you prefer, but the smaller the diameter the more hose you will need. Paint this black and either drill a hole through the middle or a shorter hole through each end to receive the hose reel axle.

5. You will find the pattern for the single-horse fills (6) in Illus. 97 page 95. Cut these out of ¼″ stock and round them with your drum sander. Paint the fills red and glue them on the body as shown. You will want to mount a singletree on the fills before assembly, but you might want to paint this a different color than the fills.

6. Buy 8′ of ¼″ vacuum hose (O) from an auto supply shop and wrap and glue it on the reel. Make the nozzle (N) from a ¼″ dowel as shown.

7. Add the springs, axle blocks, axle, and wheels shown in Chapter 6. You can use whatever size wheels you have made up on this cart.

The pattern for the driver of the horse cart is found in Illus. 105 on pages 107 and 108 along with building instructions.

The dalmatian dog could be carved too, but I got him for 19 cents at a craft shop. A couple of minutes of shaving off the mould marks and retouching the paint and the dog is ready for a ride—much easier than carving, and it's hard to tell you haven't done him all yourself.

The trotting horse pattern is in Illus. 90 page 86. It is carved like all the rest. I painted it black with lots of white markings, and harnessed it as shown in Illus. 88.

Illus. 87. Single-horse fire-hose cart.

Illus. 88. Another view of Illus. 87, in color on page E of color section.

Fire Hose Cart

Letter	Description	Quan.	Thick.	Width	Length
A	Cart sides	2	¼″	1¾″	6″
B	Seat board	1	¼″	1″	3½″
D	Footboard	1	¼″	½″	3½″
E	Floorboard	1	¼″	2″	3½″
F	Hose-reel sides	2	⅛″	2½″ dia.	
G	Hose spool	1	1½″ dia.		3″
H	Axle blocks	2	¼″	½″	½″
I	Axle	1	³⁄₁₆″ dowel		5¾″
M	Springs	4	¼″	see pattern	
N	Hose nozzle	1	see instructions		
O	Fire hose	8′ (ft)	¼″ vacuum hose—see inst.		
6	Single-horse fills see pattern Illus. 97				

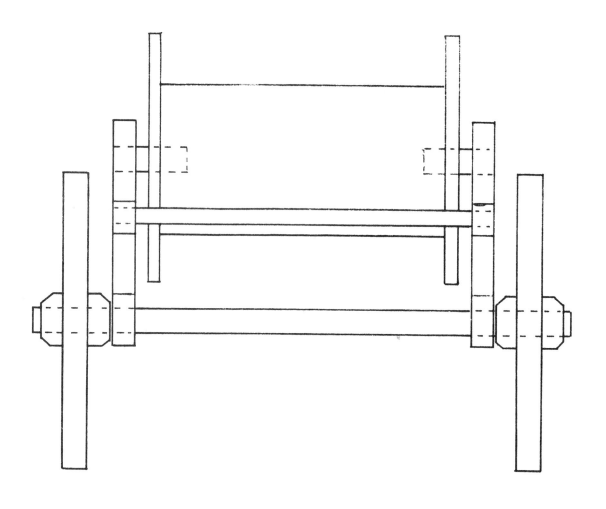

Illus. 89. Single-horse fire hose cart (full-size).

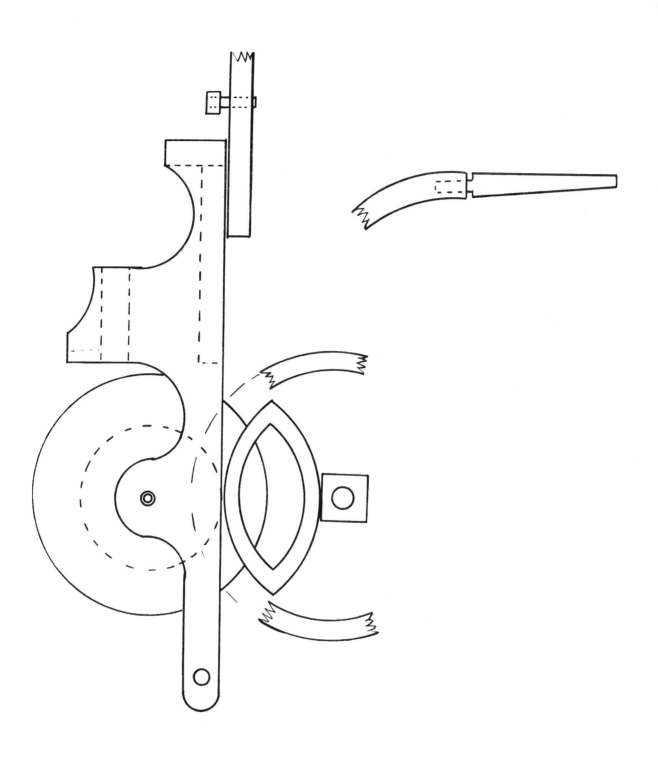

Illus. 89 *(cont.)*

Illus. 90. Trotting horse (⁸⁄₁₀″ = 1″).

8

Draft Horses, Harnesses, and Wagons

Illus. 91 and 92 are patterns of the famous Budweiser Clydesdale, one standing and one trotting. To make the draft harnesses you will need pressure-sensitive graphic tape in ⅛″ width. The letters in the following instructions refer to the harness in Illus. 91:

a. The collars are made by using cardboard or a "Copy Cat" contour gauge to make a template of your horse's neck. Use ¼″ thick wood and cut it out as shown, round it with your ½″ drum sander. You may have to cut it in two and glue it back to get it over the horse's head. Paint it whatever color you want before you put it on the horse.

b. Tape the backpad and bellyband right onto the horse as shown. Use two or three layers of tape to make the backpad appear wider and thicker.

c. Tape the breeching onto the horse. The jump ring on the breeching can be taped into the end of the rump strap as shown.

d., e., f., and g. are taped directly to the horse's head as shown. This bridle, like others, can also be painted.

h. Make the tugs 2″ to 3″ longer than you need them. Wrap them around the collar and stick the two sticky sides together. When the horse and wagon is mounted, you will cut them off just short of the singletree (1) and tape them as shown in the drawing. Use craft-shop jump rings to make chain ends on your tugs for a much better effect.

i. I made the blinds from thin pieces of wood and taped them under the headstall (f) as I was putting the bridle on.

j. I bend the bits from soft wire and then run them through the mouth. On some of them I have taped the headstall sides to each of the bit rings and then I taped them to the head so that they meet on top of the head behind the ears.

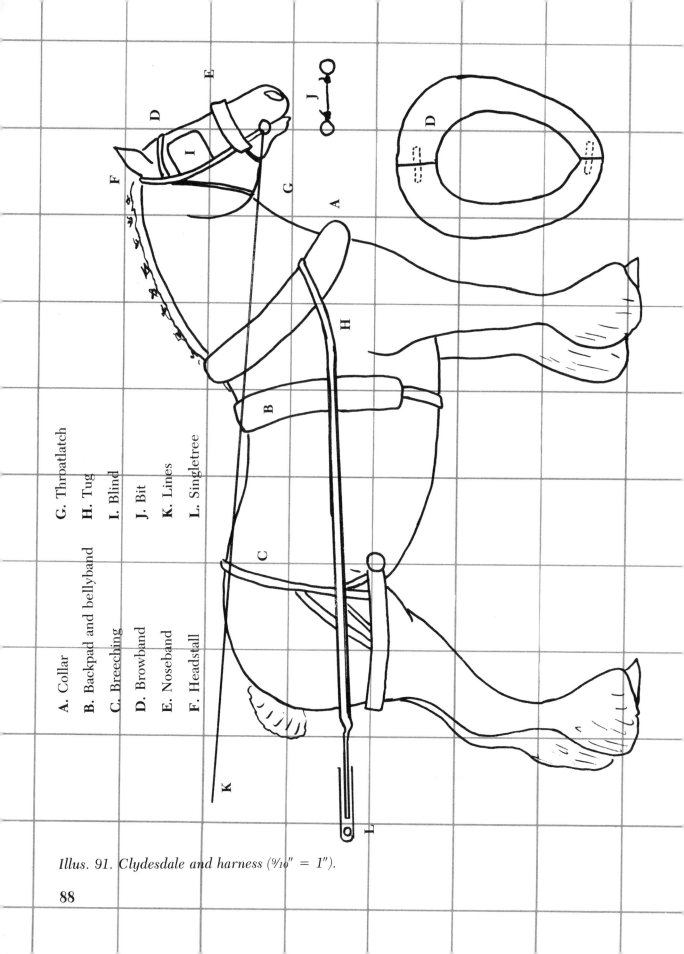

A. Collar
B. Backpad and bellyband
C. Breeching
D. Browband
E. Noseband
F. Headstall
G. Throatlatch
H. Tug
I. Blind
J. Bit
K. Lines
L. Singletree

Illus. 91. Clydesdale and harness (⁹⁄₁₀″ = 1″).

Illus. 92. Trotting Clydesdale (full-size).

Illus. 93. Two views on this page and one on facing page of steam fire-wagon. It can also be seen in color on page F of color section.

Illus. 94.

Illus. 95.

Building a Steam Fire Wagon

Urban fire departments started using horse-drawn steam-powered fire engines before 1850 and continued to use them until the 1920's. By the turn of the century there were literally hundreds of manufacturers of these popular wagons. Nearly every one was different from the others, so there are no real patterns for the most popular models. I used my fire chief's antique toy wagon for ideas and inspiration for the plans in Illus. 96, 97, and 98.

His toy had a 3-horse hitch, but the real wagons also used 2-, or 4-horse hitches. A few

were even pulled by oxen! You can use a 2-horse hitch like mine or almost any other combination of horses and be correct. The following instructions refer to the plans in the illustrations mentioned above and the description of parts on page 96; and Illus. 99 and 100.

The plans are drawn to full scale and the description of parts page has the dimensions for each part, so no parts dimensions will be given in these instructions. Start by cutting a piece of ¼" thick board 2½" wide by at least 24" long. Your seat and box-bottom boards will come off this piece. Now cut two ¼" thick boards 4" × 11½" for the sides of the box.

1. Cut the sideboards (A) Illus. 96 and 97 and drill the 3/16″ holes.
2. Cut pieces E, F, G, and H and the tailgate (does not have identifying letter in the plans) and glue them in their proper position to the sideboards. You will need clamps to hold them as they dry.
3. Cut pieces B, C, and D. When assembled and glued, glue the seat assembly to the rest of the box. On angle pieces such as the footboard (e), I make the angles on my disc sander or with the Dremel drum sanders. It is easier for me to make them oversized and sand them down to fit than to try to cut them to the right size, and I am able to get a better fit.
4. Make the fifth wheel as shown previously in Illus. 75, page 68 and glue top half (K) and (V) in place.
5. Be sure to paint the box and other completed assemblies before gluing them together in final assembly. I painted the box white and covered it with vines, borders, flowers and flags as explained earlier in the book.
6. Turn the boiler (O) and pressure tank (P) on your turning lathe. My helpful neighbor turned mine for me from these plans.
7. Cut the two cylinder housings (R) and drill the holes as shown. Insert the two piston rods (3/16″ dowels about 1 1/8″ long) in place and glue to the boiler as shown. Be sure the bottom-cylinder housing is horizontal with the bottom of the pressure tank so that the steam tube (X) will line up straight when assembled.
8. Carve the golden eagle (Q). Draw the pattern on 1/4″ stock and carve the body and wing shapes with your Dremel tools. Many of these old wagons had bells where the eagle is, and you could carve a bell here if it would be easier for you.

Paint the pressure tank (P) silver and mount the gold eagle on top.
9. Paint the boiler black with silver and gold stripes around the bands. Do not glue these to the wagon until you are sure all parts fit and you have added the other accessories to the boiler.
10. Make the relief valve (T) from 1/4″ dowel 1″ long. Shape it with your Dremel, glue the 3/32″ dowel, paint it silver and mount it on one side of the boiler (not on the back as the drawing shows).
11. Make the gauge panel (S). Cut a thin 1/8″ slice off the end of a 1/4″ dowel and two slices off the end of a 3/16″ dowel to make the gauges. Paint the panel black and the faces of the gauges white with a small line to represent the needles and glue it on the side of the boiler opposite to the pressure-relief valve. Use 2 short pieces of 3/32″ dowels to attach this so that it looks as if pipes are coming out of the boiler to the gauges.
12. Make the hand rail (U) by cutting four squares of wood 1/4″ × 1/4″ × 1/4″. Drill 3/32″ holes in these blocks—two in the ones that will be elbows and three in the ones that will be T's. Using 3/32″ dowels, cut 4 3 1/2″ for legs, 2 1 1/2″ for side rails, and 1 2 1/4″ for the front rail. Glue these together to form the hand rail and sand the elbows and T's to the proper shape with your Dremel drum sander. Paint the assembly silver and glue it in place when you make your final assembly.
13. To make the flywheels (W), I sawed 2 pieces 1/4″ thick off the end of a 1 1/2″ dowel, but these could be cut from 1/4″ stock if you do not have the dowel. With a 1″ spade bit I drilled a hole half-way through the wheels and glued a 1/2″ long piece of 3/16″ dowel in the hole left by the

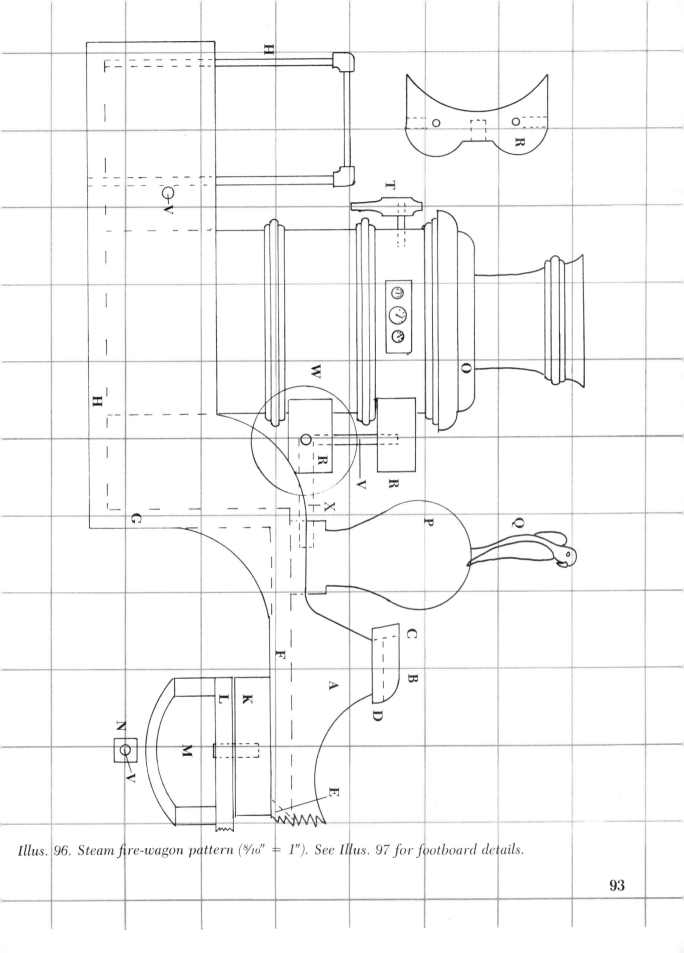

Illus. 96. Steam fire-wagon pattern (⁸/₁₀″ = 1″). *See Illus. 97 for footboard details.*

93

spade bit. Paint the flywheels red, then paint the recessed part white and with your stylus make a row of dots around the outside of the rim. Insert and glue the flywheel axles in the holes in the cylinder housings on the boiler.

14. These wagons always seemed to have a starter piece of hose 3' to 4' long mounted on the side. You will notice these pieces of hose in the photographs (Illus. 93, 94 and 95). The plans do not show this hose, but number (4) in Illus. 98 is a pattern for the brackets for this hose. Make the brackets from the pattern, paint them red and glue them on the side of your box. Now paint a 3" length of ³⁄₁₆" dowel black with ¼" of each end painted silver to represent metal threaded ends on the hose. Make one hose for each side and glue in place in the brackets.

15. Number (5) in Illus. 98 is the wagon's hose coupling. Make 2 of these from a ¼" dowel and a ³⁄₁₆" dowel as shown and glue them in holes (Y), Illus. 97 after you have painted them silver.

16. The rest of the wagon is described in Chapter 6 starting on page 64. This would be the axles, wheels, springs, fifth wheels, tongue, neck yoke, and double-trees etc.

17. Glue all assemblies together and mount the wagon and horses on your baseboard and cut the tongue to proper length.

18. You will find patterns for the firemen on pages 107 and 108.

Note: The best thing I have found for lines is called "posi wire." It is very soft yet stays in position from the horse to the driver and gives a look of being real. I like to leave 2 or 3 inches flying out behind the driver's hands.

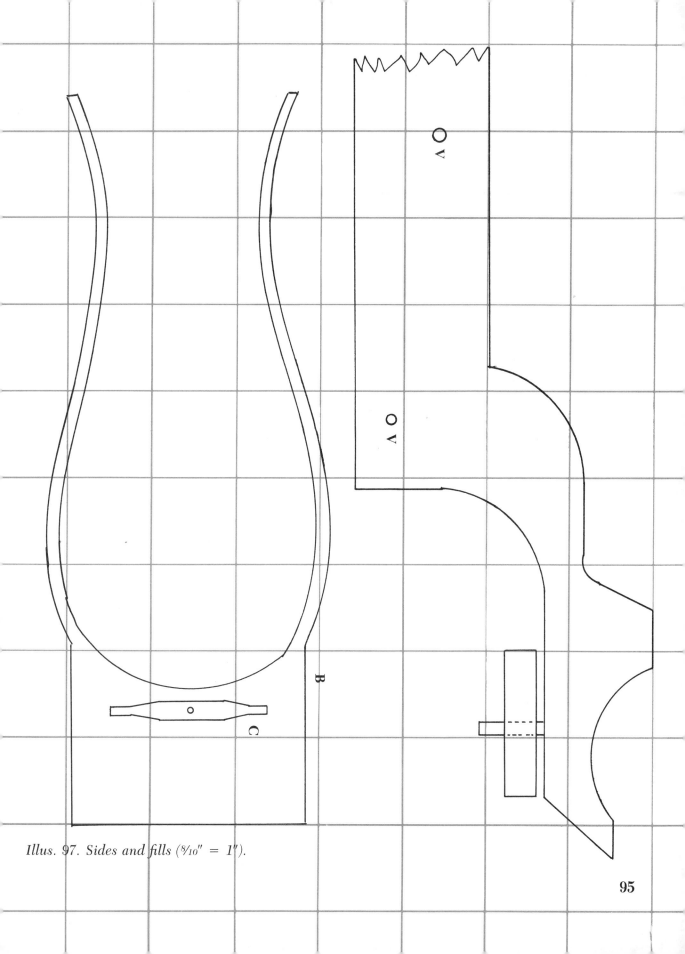

Illus. 97. Sides and fills (⁸/₁₀″ = 1″).

STEAM FIRE WAGON

Letter	Description	Quan.	Thick.	Width	Length
A	Wagon box side	2	¼″	4″	11½″
B	Seat side	2	¼″	½″	1¼″
C	Seat back	1	¼″	½″	2½″
D	Seat board	1	¼″	1″	2½″
E	Foot board	1	¼″	1⅜″	2½″
F	Box bottom - front	1	¼″	2½″	4¼″
G	Box bottom - vertical	1	¼″	2½″	2½″
H	Box bottom - rear	1	¼″	2½″	6⅛″
	Tailgate	1	¼″	1¾″	2½″
I	4″ wheel	2			
J	3″ wheel	2			
K	Top fifth wheel	1	½″	2″ diameter	
L	Bottom fifth wheel	1	¼″	See pattern	
M	Springs	4	¼″	See pattern	
N	Axle	1	½″	½″	4″
O	Boiler	1		3″ od	6¾″
P	Pressure tank	1		1½″ od	2½″
Q	Golden eagle	1	¼″	2¼″	2¼″
R	Cylinder housings	2	½″	1¼″	2″
S	Gauge panel	1	¼″	½″	1″
T	Relief valve	1			
U	Hand rails	1			
V	³⁄₁₆″ dowels (or holes)	7	³⁄₆″	various	
W	Flywheels	2	¼″	1½″ diam.	
X	Steam tube	1	¼″ dowel		1¼″
1.	Evener	1	¼″	⅜″	3″
2.	Doubletree	2	¼″	¼″	2″
3.	Neck yoke	1	¼″	½″	2½″
4.	Hose brackets	2	¼″	see pattern & inst.	
5.	Hose connection	2	see inst.		
6. 7.	Tongue	1	see inst.		

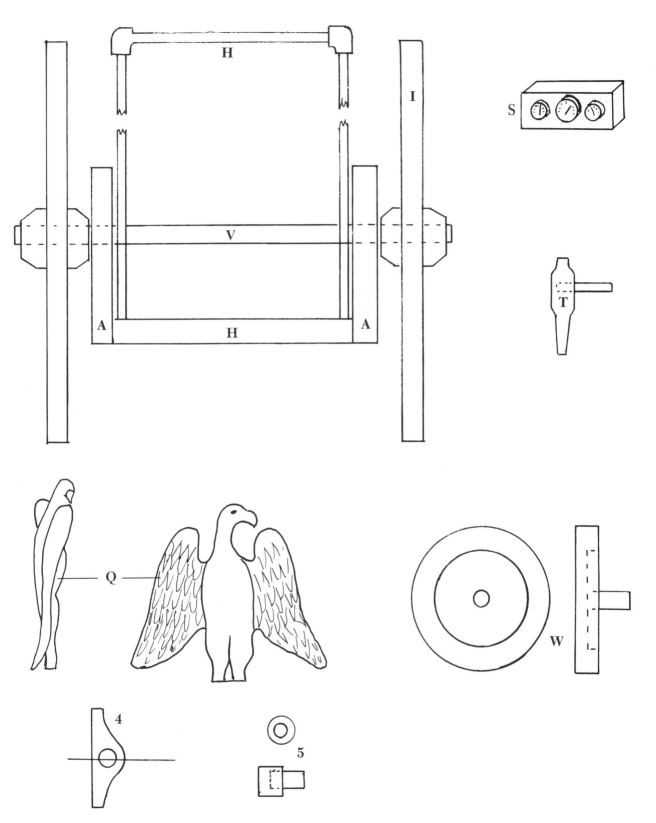

Illus. 98. Steam fire wagon parts.

Illus. 99.

Illus. 100. The two illustrations on this page can be seen in color on page H of the color section.

Illus. 101. Close-up view of wagon.

Building a Fire Ladder Wagon

Once the steam-powered pumps were put on wagons and pulled by horses the urban fire departments needed a fast way to get their ladders and men to the fires. Horses were the natural way, so a multitude of different wagons were made for this purpose. Since the wagons had to be long and the streets were often very narrow, many were built with tiller

been incorporated in these plans. The tiller wheel and driver adds interest.

I made the bed 15″ long. It could be a little shorter or longer, but this seems to be in pretty good scale, as you can see from the photos. The page size of this book does not let me show full scale on the length of the wagon, but the rest of the parts are draw full scale, and you can get measurements from the plans or the parts description page. The following building instructions refer to the plans on pages 101, 104, and 105.

don't look manufactured.

forms for the firemen to ride on, and one has

1. Cut a board ¼″ × 2″ × 24″. From this board cut the box bottom (U) 15″ long and cut the seat parts B, C, D, E, F, and G from the balance of the 2″ wide board. Cut the tiller driver's seat sides (X).

2. Cut the 2 side boards (A) and glue them to the bottom (U).

3. Glue the seat together from the parts cut in 1. above and glue the seat assembly to the sideboards. *Be sure* to locate and drill the 3 ³⁄₃₂″ holes in each of the seat sides (C) and (X) before gluing the seats together. These will support ladders and need to be lined up properly.

4. To make the 3 ladder-bracket assemblies (H) start by cutting a board ¼″ × ¼″ × at least 8″. From this board cut 6 pieces 1⅛″ long. Mark and drill the ³⁄₃₂″ holes as shown on (H). Drill them in pairs so the holes line up. Next cut 9 pieces of ³⁄₃₂″ dowels at least 2½″ long. These will be glued into the holes just drilled. When gluing these 3 assemblies together be sure that the out-to-out width is the same as your wagon bed, so that they can be glued onto the top of the bed sides (A). *Note:* The drawing shows only 2 of these assemblies because of space. Glue the seats and ladder brackets to the box sides.

5. Spray-paint the box assembly red, border it with a fine-point permanent pen in black, and fill in all areas with vines and flowers.

6. Make the 2 firemen's platform supports (Q) from the patterns and paint red.

7. The firemen's platform (R) is shown as ¼″ thick, but I made mine from ⅛″ stock; and I think it looks better and is plenty stout. Paint this red and border the top side black. Glue it to the brackets (O) and the brackets to the bottom of the box bed (A) as shown.

8. Make the tiller wheel (I), shaft (P), pillow blocks (S), and gear box (T) from the plans. Paint the wheel red, the shaft silver, and the pillow blocks and gear box black and glue the assembly to the right-hand side of the driver's seat as shown. Put some silver dots on the gear box to represent bolts.

9. The 2 fire axes are cut to shape from a ¼″ piece of scrap, the handle hole ³⁄₃₂″ is drilled and the head is then sanded to shape with the Dremel drum. Glue a ³⁄₃₂″ dowel in for a handle, paint the axe red and white and mount one on each side of the tiller driver's seat.

10. To make the leather buckets (leather is what they used for many years) I cut 1″ pieces off a ¾″ dowel and drilled out the center. The bails are a length of soft wire pushed into 2 small holes near the top of the pail. With the end of a ½″ drum sander, I made Xs on one side to represent stitches in the leather. I hung 3 on each side of the box by gluing short pieces of ³⁄₃₂″ dowels in at a slight angle. Paint the buckets brown.

11. The ladder racks will hold 4 16″ ladders (O) and the firemen's platform will hold 2 about 7″ long. I also made 1 with wire hooks that is about 4″ long and lays up on top of the top ladder. All the ladders are made the same. Cut about 14 feet of ¼″ × ¼″ wood then cut to lengths—8 16″, 4 7″, and 2 4″.

Put a guide fence on your drill press and set it so that the holes are centered on ¼″. Be sure to drill a pair of rails at a time so that the holes line up. Starting 1″ from one end drill your first hole. Push a ³⁄₃₂″ food-skewer dowel through this hole so the rails stay aligned while you continue to drill holes every 1″ the length of the

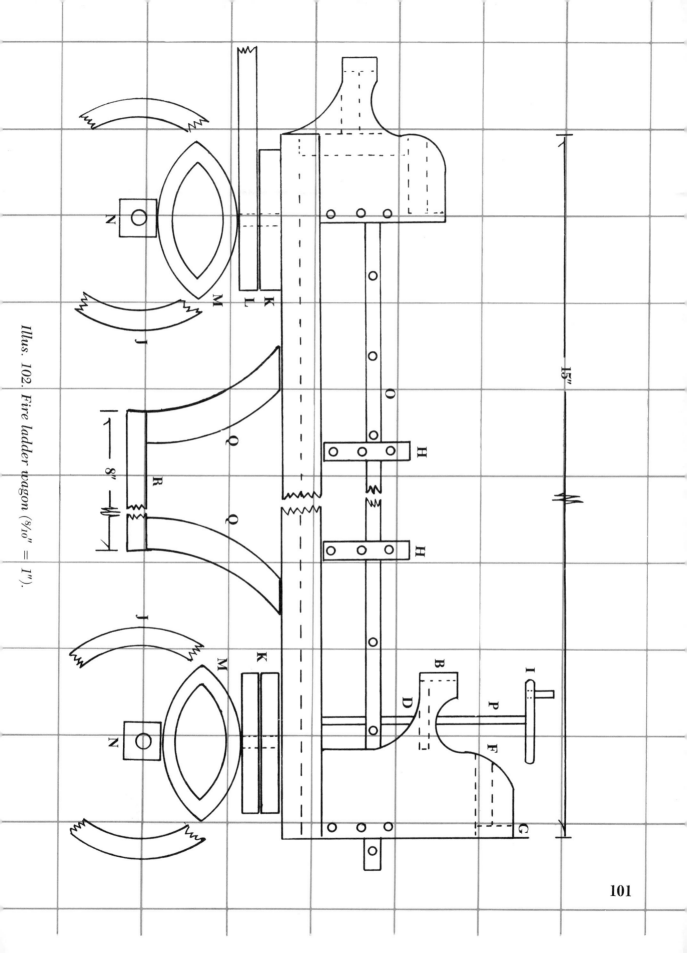

Illus. 102. Fire ladder wagon (8/10" = 1").

rail. You can make a mark on your fence guide 1" from the drill bit and just line the previous hole drilled up with this mark to get your next hole location.

When all your ladder rails are drilled and sanded (on what will be the inside of the rail for sure), cut enough of the 3/32" dowels 2¼" long to complete your ladders. Cut 2 pieces of scrap wood ¼" × 1⅜" × 3" to 4" to use as spacers between the 2 rails while you are gluing the rungs in place. Before you start gluing be sure that these spacer strips are the right width so that the ladders will slide freely into the ladder brackets.

Assemble and glue the ladders together, sand the ends of the rungs smooth, spray-paint them white and then add some "curly Qs" on the outside of each rail with a fine point permanent black pen. I painted "B. J. LADDER CO." on the center of each of mine, and you may want to do the same with your name. It gets smiles.

12. When your horses are carved from Illus. 104 you will find the collar and harness plans starting on page 88.
13. The hand rails for the firemen to hang onto when they are on the platform is not shown in the plans. To make these, simply make 6 pillow blocks like the ones shown as (S) in Illus. 102. Drill 3/32" holes, glue one onto each of the ladder brackets (H) and put a 3/32" dowel connecting them. The pillow blocks should be black and the rail silver.
14. The rest of the wagon is described in Chapter 6.
15. You will find patterns for the firemen in Illus. 105, pages 107 and 108.

LADDER WAGON

Letter	Description	Quan.	Thick	Width	Length
A	Wagon Box Sides	2	1/4″	1/2″	15″
B	Foot Board	2	1/4″	1/2″	2″
C	Seat Sides	2	1/4″	2 1/4″	2 1/4″
D	Floorboard	2	1/4″	1″	2″
E	Seat Front	1	1/4″	1 3/8″	2″
F	Seat Board	2	1/4″	1″	2″
G	Seat Back	2	1/8″	1/2″	2″
H	Ladder bracket assem.	3	see patterns & instructions		
I	Tiller Steering Wheel	1	1/8″	1″ diameter	
J	Wheels (can use size in inv.)	4	see wheel plans		
K	Fifth Wheels	3	1/4″	1 3/4″ diameter	
L	Fifth Wheel	1	see pattern for 1 3/4″		
M	Springs	8	see spring pattern		
N	Axle	2	1/2″	1/2″	4″
O	Ladders		see building instructions		
P	Tiller steering shaft	1	1/8″ dowel		
Q	Fireman's platform supports	2	see building instructions		
R	Fireman's Platform	1	1/4″	4 1/4″	8″
S	Pillow Blocks	2	1/4″	1/2″	3/4″
T	Gear Box	1	1/2″	1/2″	1/2″
U	Wagon Box Floor	1	1/4″	2″	15″
W	Hand Rail Brackets	6	1/4″	see pattern & inst. 2 1/4″	2 1/2″
X	Tiller Driver's Seat Sides	2	1/4″	see pattern	

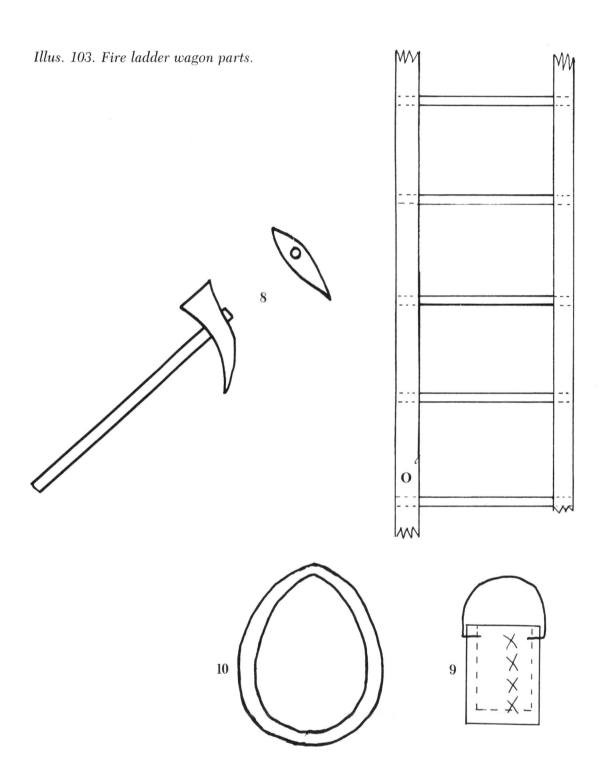

Illus. 103. Fire ladder wagon parts.

8

O

10

9

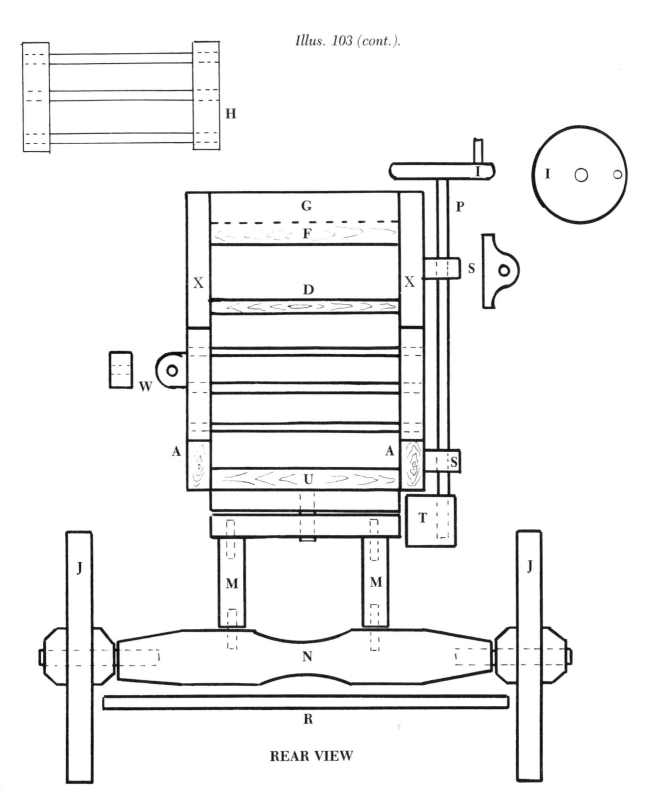

Illus. 103 (cont.).

H

G

F

X   X

D

I

P

S

W

A   A

U

S

T

M   M

J   J

N

R

REAR VIEW

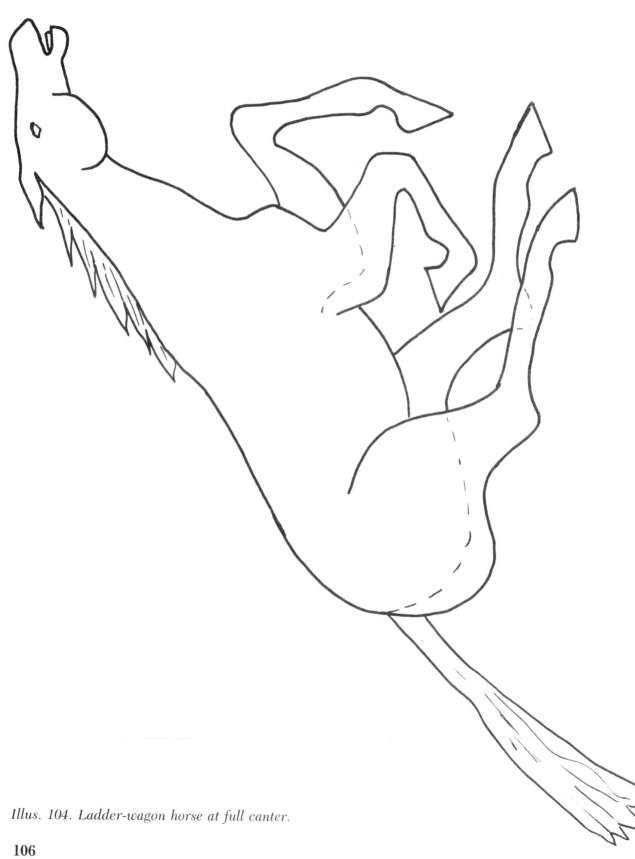

Illus. 104. Ladder-wagon horse at full canter.

106

Carving Passengers

Illus. 105 contains patterns of firemen in various positions. They will work in other places with minor adjustments. Make your patterns on tracing paper and fit them to the seat they are going to be on—you may have to change leg length, etc. It is not uncommon to have to sand the rumps some to make them fit in the seats and have their feet touch where you want them.

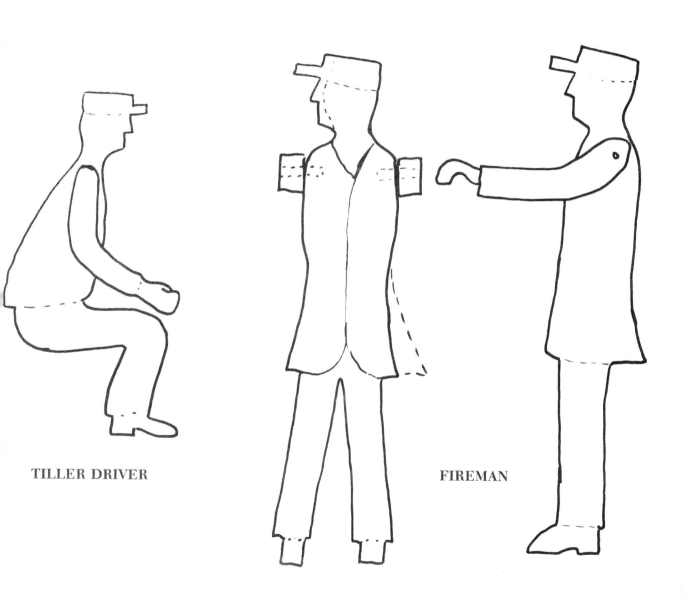

TILLER DRIVER

FIREMAN

Illus. 105. Firemen.

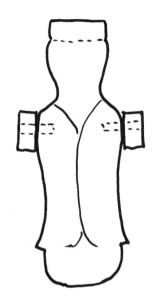

BACKS AND FRONTS

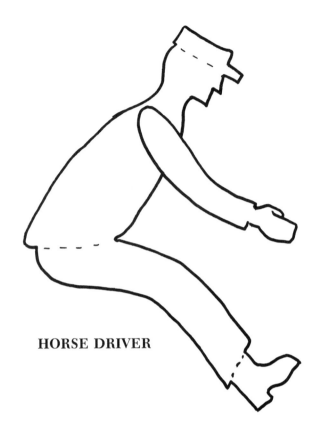

HORSE DRIVER

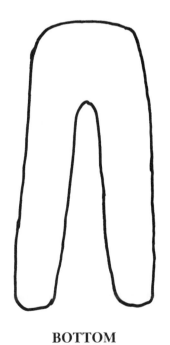

BOTTOM

Illus. 105 (cont.)

108

1. I rough-saw the hats, heads, bodies, and legs from one chunk of scrap wood. Then the arms and heads are rough-sawn to shape and later fastened to the body with a short $3/32''$ dowel.

2. I use a Dremel $1/2''$ drum sander and round the entire figure—hat, head, body, and legs except at the shoulders. When the body is nearly where I want it and usually after the face is carved in (see 3 below), I glue the rough-cut arms in the positions I need to fit the application. It is easiest to carve the hands before gluing the arms in place. Now you can round and blend the shoulders to the body.

3. To make the face, I use a Dremel #121 acorn cutter. Cut the eye-socket areas down evenly, then shape the nose, mouth, jaw, and neck areas. I then use a grinding stone (like the Dremel #952) to grind the face smooth. I paint the face, neck, hands, and any exposed flesh a Caucasian flesh color and just use dots for eyes and mouths. You can make some shallow lines in the hair area and paint the hair whatever color you want. You can paint the uniforms whatever color you want. My firemen's uniforms are black trimmed in silver. The beer-wagon driver has a green uniform trimmed in red and black and has a white cap. Race-sulky drivers can be any colors you choose.

Some carving notes. The cost fronts are shallow lines as drawn in #4 in Illus. 105 and are made with the end of a $1/2''$ drum sander or #121 Dremel acorn cutter.

Number 2 is for a man looking to his left or right. You can make your man look either way or straight ahead by turning the tracing paper. The men riding on the ladder wagon should be looking ahead. For these you should use the dotted line on the drawing to make the coat appear like it is flying back in the wind.

I bought the book *Whittlin' Bill's Folk Characters* by Bill Higginbotham, published by Sterling Publishing Co., Inc., New York and got a lot of help with features, hands, beards, etc., from it. A copy of this book and his other book, *Whittling*, (Sterling Publishing Co., Inc., New York) would be very helpful to you, too.

Building a Beer Wagon

A friend of mine is a partner in a new Micro-Brewery restaurant in Chicago. It is built in an old warehouse with brick walls and high ceilings and the decor is turn-of-the-century. He asked me to build a beer wagon and hitch that would add to the decor but would not be a copy of the famous Budweiser hitch.

Several hours in the library told me that many smaller brewers have or still are using horse hitches on beer wagons to promote their products. All beer wagons are similar, but each seems to have its own identifying characteristics. Without copying any one but drawing from many photos, I drew and built this wagon (Illus. 106–108).

So the horses would each look different and still be a matched teams, I made patterns for two different horses. They are both cantering, but the head sets and leg positions are changed. After they were sawed out on the bandsaw, I marked the legs out on different sides so that they are all out of step; and as you can see in the photos, they look very natural.

Illus. 106. Beer wagon and Clydesdales.

The tails are also all flying in different direc- tions. The patterns for the horses are in Illus. 110 and 111. You can see in the photos that they are painted jet black with lots of socks and strips in their faces. The harnesses were made with green tape to give them a little

Illus. 107. Different view; can also be seen in color on page G of color section.

Illus. 108. Close-up view of beer wagon. In color on page G of color section.

more color. You will find the collar and harness plans and instructions starting on page 88.

The following instructions refer to the letters and parts descriptions in the table on page 104 and Illus. 109. Measurements of the various parts can be taken from the descriptions or measured on the plans:

1. Use double-sided transparent tape and cut both sides (A) at one time.
2. Make the floor (B).
3. Make the 8 sideboard braces (C). Cut these about a ¼″ long so that you can sand the top ends off at a 45-degree angle and sand the bottom end to the correct length. This is easier than trying to cut them to just the right length. These will represent 2″ × 4″ braces.
4. Make the 4 sideboard braces (D) a little long so that you can sand them down to the correct length when you get ready to assemble. On your belt or disc sander taper the top edge (2″ way) to 45 degrees so the flare boards (E) will fit.
5. Make the flareboards (E) and 45 degree them top and bottom as shown in the rear view in fig. 112.

6. Cut the seat parts F, G, H, I, and O to dimensions shown.

7. Assemble and glue all of the box parts that you have made.

8. Cut the 5 floorboard braces (Q). These represent 2″ × 4″ horizontal braces that are found on almost all wagons. Round the ends of these and drill a small hole in each end to receive the wire braces (no number in the drawings), which you will be putting on in the final assembly after the box is painted. Glue the floorboard braces (Q) directly under the vertical side braces (C). You can drill a small hole in the (C) braces about ½″ up from the bottom to receive the wire braces talked about earlier.

9. I added a vertical and horizontal board on each side of the driver's seat to frame in two 1″ × 1″ craft shop mirrors. You can see these mirrors in the photos.

10. I painted the box white, put red border lines on all areas and painted vines and flowers wherever there was room. The American flags are decals I found in a model airplane store.

11. I made the brake assembly (P) from the plans and glued it so that the brake pads just cleared the wheels after they were assembled.

12. The axles, wheels, tongues, and neck yokes and doubletrees were painted yellow and trimmed in red. The springs were painted black. These are all described in Chapter 6, starting on page 64.

13. The round frames around the beer company logo were made like a wheel rim is made in fig. 71 pages 64 and 65. After it was glued back together, we cut a bead around it with my neighbor's Dremel router attachment and painted it yellow.

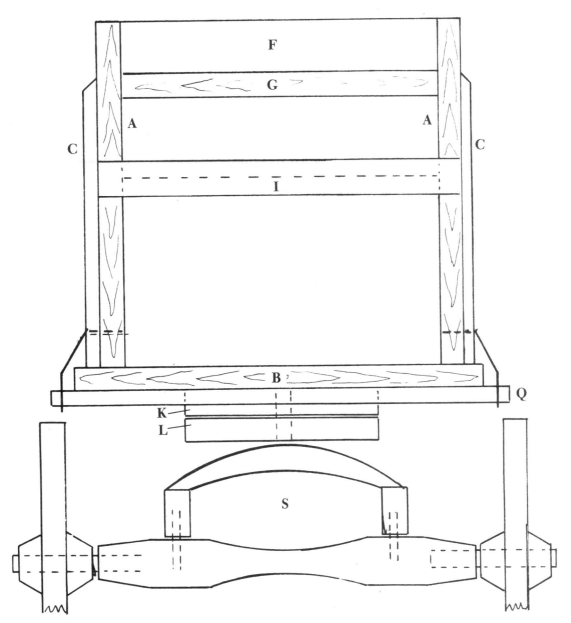

Illus. 109. Front view of beer wagon (full-size pattern).

BEER WAGON

Letter	Description	Quan.	Thick.	Width	Length
A	Box sides	2	1/4″	3¼″	11½″
B	Floor board	1	1/4″	4¼″	10″
C	Sideboard braces	8	1/8″	1/4″	1⅞″
D	Sideboard braces	4	1/8″	1/4″	2″
E	Flare boards	4	1/8″	3/4″	2½″
F	Seat back	1	1/4″	3¼″	3½″
G	Seat board	1	1/4″	1″	3¼″
H	Seat front	1	1/4″	2¾″	3¼″
I	Foot board	1	1/4″	7/8″	3¼″
L	Fifth wheel	1			
K	Fifth wheel	1	1/4″	2″ diam.	
N	Axles	2	1/2″	1/2″	4″
O	Footboard	1	1/4″	1/2″	3¼″
P	Break pads	2	1/4″	3/8″	1″
Q	Floorboard braces	5	1/8″	1/4″	4¾″
S	Springs	8	1/4″ see pattern & instructions		
T	Brake shaft arm supports	2	1/4″	1/4″	1½″

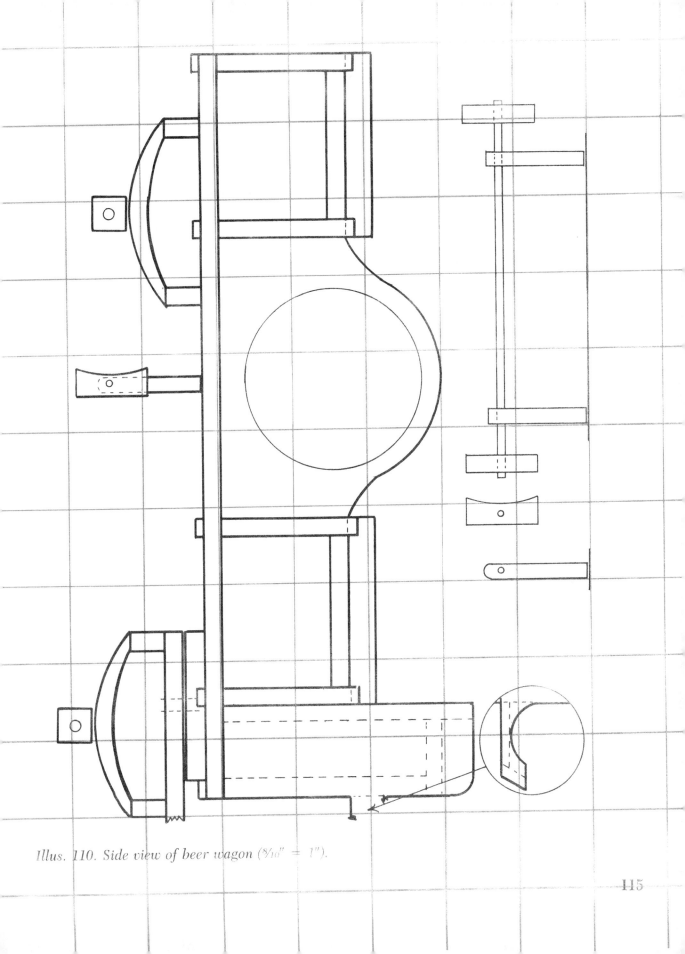

Illus. 110. Side view of beer wagon ($\frac{5}{16}$" = 1").

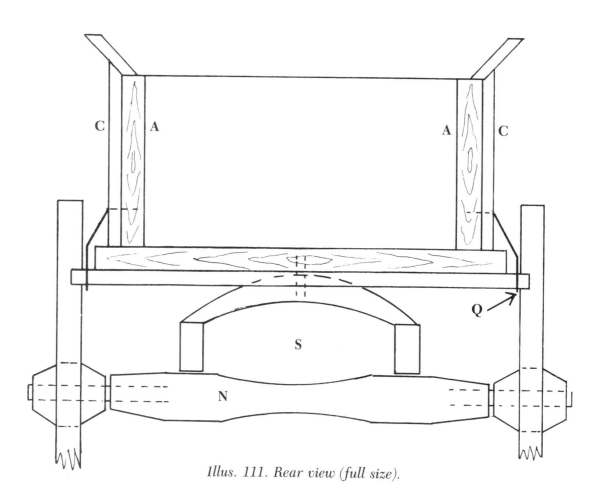

Illus. 111. Rear view (full size).

Illus. 112. Clydesdale.

117

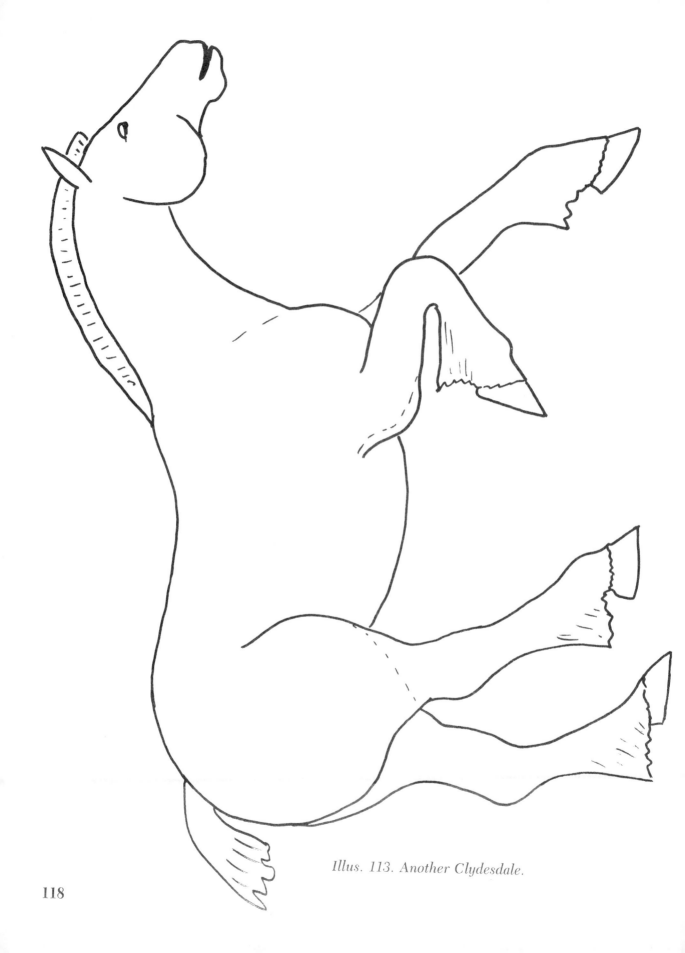

Illus. 113. Another Clydesdale.

Appendices

About the Author

Billy J. Smith was born and raised in Lamont, Iowa, where, at 16 years of age, he started selling agricultural equipment. Married to Doris in 1948, they and their three children lived in Illinois, Wisconsin, and Nebraska, where he worked as a salesman and sales manager before returning to Nashua, Iowa, as a founding partner of Skyline Harvestore Systems, Inc. in 1965.

Mr. Smith authored and published a sales manual entitled *The Billy J. Book* and for several years he held sales seminars nationwide to train salespeople to use the manual and its revisions.

During this period he became a popular banquet speaker and talked at local, county, state, and national agricultural meetings and conventions.

In 1981, he sold his successful business and retired to Mesa, Arizona, and a summer home at Delhi, Iowa, where he plays golf, carves, builds furniture, and now has written another book.

Bibliography

Here are some of the good books that I have found to be an inspiration for designs and methods. You can probably find them (and many more) in your local book shop or library.

Fraley, Tobin, *The Carousel Animal* (1983) Zephyr Press, P.O. Box 3066, Berkeley, CA 94703.

Higginbotham, Bill, *Whittling* (1982) Sterling Publishing Co., Inc., 387 Park Avenue South, New York, NY 10016.

Higginbotham, Bill, *Whittlin' Bill's Folk Characters* (1985) Sterling Publishing Co., Inc., 387 Park Avenue South, New York, NY 10016.

Manns, William and Peggy Shank, *Painted Ponies* (1986) Zon International Publishing Co., P.O. Box 47, Millwood, NY 10546.

Price, Steven D., *All the King's Horses*, Viking Press, 40 West 23rd Street, New York, NY 10010.

METRIC EQUIVALENCY CHART

MM—MILLIMETRES   CM—CENTIMETRES

INCHES TO MILLIMETRES AND CENTIMETRES

INCHES	MM	CM	INCHES	CM	INCHES	CM
⅛	3	0.3	9	22.9	30	76.2
¼	6	0.6	10	25.4	31	78.7
⅜	10	1.0	11	27.9	32	81.3
½	13	1.3	12	30.5	33	83.8
⅝	16	1.6	13	33.0	34	86.4
¾	19	1.9	14	35.6	35	88.9
⅞	22	2.2	15	38.1	36	91.4
1	25	2.5	16	40.6	37	94.0
1¼	32	3.2	17	43.2	38	96.5
1½	38	3.8	18	45.7	39	99.1
1¾	44	4.4	19	48.3	40	101.6
2	51	5.1	20	50.8	41	104.1
2½	64	6.4	21	53.3	42	106.7
3	76	7.6	22	55.9	43	109.2
3½	89	8.9	23	58.4	44	111.8
4	102	10.2	24	61.0	45	114.3
4½	114	11.4	25	63.5	46	116.8
5	127	12.7	26	66.0	47	119.4
6	152	15.2	27	68.6	48	121.9
7	178	17.8	28	71.1	49	124.5
8	203	20.3	29	73.7	50	127.0

YARDS TO METRES

YARDS	METRES	YARDS	METRES	YARDS	METRES	YARDS	METRES	YARDS	METRES
⅛	0.11	2⅛	1.94	4⅛	3.77	6⅛	5.60	8⅛	7.43
¼	0.23	2¼	2.06	4¼	3.89	6¼	5.72	8¼	7.54
⅜	0.34	2⅜	2.17	4⅜	4.00	6⅜	5.83	8⅜	7.66
½	0.46	2½	2.29	4½	4.11	6½	5.94	8½	7.77
⅝	0.57	2⅝	2.40	4⅝	4.23	6⅝	6.06	8⅝	7.89
¾	0.69	2¾	2.51	4¾	4.34	6¾	6.17	8¾	8.00
⅞	0.80	2⅞	2.63	4⅞	4.46	6⅞	6.29	8⅞	8.12
1	0.91	3	2.74	5	4.57	7	6.40	9	8.23
1⅛	1.03	3⅛	2.86	5⅛	4.69	7⅛	6.52	9⅛	8.34
1¼	1.14	3¼	2.97	5¼	4.80	7¼	6.63	9¼	8.46
1⅜	1.26	3⅜	3.09	5⅜	4.91	7⅜	6.74	9⅜	8.57
1½	1.37	3½	3.20	5½	5.03	7½	6.86	9½	8.69
							7⅞	7.32	10	9.14

Index